David Candela
Hugo Vega

Knowledge Management for Software Production

AF209960

David Candela
Hugo Vega

Knowledge Management for Software Production

Knowledge Management for Specialized Software Production in a University Computer Lab

ScienciaScripts

Imprint

Any brand names and product names mentioned in this book are subject to trademark, brand or patent protection and are trademarks or registered trademarks of their respective holders. The use of brand names, product names, common names, trade names, product descriptions etc. even without a particular marking in this work is in no way to be construed to mean that such names may be regarded as unrestricted in respect of trademark and brand protection legislation and could thus be used by anyone.

Cover image: www.ingimage.com

This book is a translation from the original published under ISBN 978-620-2-81000-5.

Publisher:
Sciencia Scripts
is a trademark of
Dodo Books Indian Ocean Ltd. and OmniScriptum S.R.L publishing group

120 High Road, East Finchley, London, N2 9ED, United Kingdom
Str. Armeneasca 28/1, office 1, Chisinau MD-2012, Republic of Moldova, Europe
Managing Directors: Ieva Konstantinova, Victoria Ursu
info@omniscriptum.com

Printed at: see last page
ISBN: 978-620-2-87064-1

Dedication

I have a lot of affection for my University and in particular for the Faculties of Systems Engineering and Computer Science, which gave me the opportunity to do this thesis and train me professionally; although I did not train in the first one mentioned, it comes from the School where I studied and where several of my professors and several fellow students came, now professors with whom we once and at some point shared university environments.

Acknowledgements

My deepest and widest gratitude goes to all those people who in one way or another encouraged me to take up and go forward in the achievement of this objective, mainly to those who had a direct commitment to this work such as the guidance, help and advice received in the definition, preparation and achievement of this Thesis and especially to my mother for giving me the example and instilling in me from a very young age the importance of study in life and to my father for his admirable intelligence and great ability to earn a living and his tireless work and commendable effort in the support and welfare of our family. At the risk of forgetting someone, I will mention the people who in one way or another influenced the realization of this work: Professor Abigail Ibañez, the first person who gave me the opportunity to venture into university teaching and who trusted me from the beginning, taught me that all circles must be closed and that it was not enough to have graduate studies because it was necessary to obtain a Master's degree; now I am sure she was not wrong with me and what she said, may God rest her soul. To my Master's Thesis advisor Dr. Hugo Vega for his extraordinary simplicity and his willingness to accept my request for advice at a time when several people were turning away from my request. To the directives, advice, corrections, observations and help of Professor Virginia Vera for having guided me correctly in the establishment and "landing" in the subject of my thesis. To all the professors who provided me with access to their classrooms for the respective surveys that support this research such as Jaime Pariona, Walter Contreras, Luzmila Pro, Gustavo Arredondo, Juan Carlos Gonzales Suarez, Marcos Sotelo, Hugo Vega, Luz Del Pino, Luis Angel Guerra, William Henríquez, Jorge Díaz, Santiago Moquillaza, Augusto Cortez and all those appreciated students who collaborated very seriously with this survey and in whose faces I could perceive that hunger for knowledge and that desire to forge a profession very typical of San Marcos' students.. To Professor Daniel Quinto and Luzmila Pro for their observations, suggestions and corrections to my thesis as part of the corresponding reporting jury, and finally my deepest thanks to all my English teachers at the San Marcos Language Center who helped me to know a little more about English and to master it better in order to successfully take the proficiency exam and obtain the certificate of foreign language proficiency required to support the master's thesis. Thanks for being so demanding, they made me relive my time as an undergraduate student.

Table of Contents

List of figures

List of tables

Summary

This study examined the knowledge management methods and tools that were applied in a computer laboratory for software production; this study was applied to male and female students of the School of Systems and Computer Engineering of all cycles who participated in a laboratory course where software was developed. It was an exploratory research of quantitative type; systematic observation and a questionnaire were used. Three hypotheses were tested whose results indicated a very tenuous identification in the use and knowledge of some method and tool of knowledge management for the production of software; therefore, it was concluded that students were not very familiar with some method or tool of knowledge management to produce software in a computer laboratory, and it was not determined a specific and massive production of software and it did not determine a standard didactic strategy for the produced software.

Keywords: ICT tools, knowledge management methodologies, knowledge management tools, computer lab, software production.

Introduction

No background equal to this research has been found, however, there is much comment on the importance of the implementation of knowledge management in all areas and mainly in the higher academic environment, especially to improve processes and to be able to generate and make better use of the information and knowledge that each element of an organization has, be these units, departments, objects and people. The objective of this study is to determine which knowledge management methods and tools are applied in a computer laboratory to generate software. What we want to know mainly, besides which methods could be used, was if some tools are specifically used such as a history of results, a documentary database or a directory of experts. This study is justified by the objective of producing specialized software that has utility and applicability not only for the university but for the community in general. This study was conducted at the Faculty of Systems Engineering and Computer Science of San Marcos University during the month of November 2018. The biggest limitation was not being able to be present during the academic activities in one of the laboratories, due to the refusal or discomfort of the professors responsible, however, students participating in a laboratory course where software was produced, had access to the classrooms during some theoretical class. We consider this study of academic and professional utility since the Faculty could achieve a specialization and strength in software development, in addition our graduates would have a unique professional competence that would allow them to be inserted in the labor field in specific activities of high specialization.

Chapter 1 describes the current situation of software production in the Faculty, and also states the objectives, justification and viability.
Chapter 2 contains the background, theoretical references, hypotheses, and variables studied.

Chapter 3 describes the methodology used, the population, the sample size, and the research and data collection technique.

Chapter 4 analyzes, interprets and describes the results of the research based on the indicators studied and represents them graphically.

This study concludes that no knowledge management method or tool is clearly and specifically identified to produce software in a computer lab at the San Marcos School of Systems and Computer Engineering.

Chapter 1. Problematic situation

During the time as an undergraduate and graduate student, software development was more than a planned, integral process, with a clear, ambitious and profitable objective not only for the student but also for the academic school and society in a suicidal adventure that could lead us to fail the course if we did not demonstrate knowledge of the instructions and syntax of a programming language applied to the solution of any practical case; and the perception that we had the students of this fact was only to approve the course demonstrating to have learned to use the instructions and the syntax of a programming language without any objective to future, neither professionally nor academically; In other words, it was not useful in the workplace if the company where you started working was not going to use it or if the programming language learned during the course was not useful to automate some administrative process of the school, faculty or university; or in the best case scenario, that it would be useful to the other generations of students to reuse those modules to create one that has some practical application and is extensive to society or has an application in the educational, commercial or industrial field.

We are experiencing a dizzying knowledge era that forces us to do things differently and to uproot ourselves from the traditional way in which things are being done, mainly in the university environment, and for this reason a change of mentality is needed to adapt the functional and legislative framework to be able to adapt the university system to the demands and requirements of today's society and to take advantage of the skills with which the new students are imbued together with the teaching methodologies and ICT tools.

1.1. Problem Formulation

Research objectives: This research aims to determine what knowledge management methods and tools are used to produce software in the computer labs of the School of Systems and Computer Engineering at San Marcos University.

Some research questions:

- What is implicit knowledge?
- What is explicit knowledge?
- What knowledge management tools have you used for software production in your lab sessions?
- have you used a history of results in your lab sessions?
- Have you used a documentary database in your lab sessions?
- have you made use of a directory of experts in your lab sessions?

Justification of the research: the convenience of the research lies in the fact that it seeks to produce software based on knowledge management processes that help to extend its application and usefulness to the university community and the community in general, which can solve problems and meet demands, mainly in the field of virtual simulation. This would also strengthen the creation of specialized software with clear production rules and objectives, seeking that the Faculty finds its own strength in software production in some activity that meets the needs of the University or the market.

Feasibility of the research: for the realization of this research it is not necessary significant financial resources since the activities will be directed to the students who take laboratory courses where software is developed at the Faculty of Systems Engineering and Computer Science of the University of San Marcos to which they have free access and know several professors who could facilitate access to their group of students to whom they will apply a survey and there will be a process of nonparticipatory or external observation. On the part of the human resources there are also no inconveniences because the realization of all the activities will be in charge of the researcher himself and which does not demand more than one person, and in the case of the materials to be used they are not expensive due to the use of survey sheets, mobility, data analysis software and a PC for the operational part. The time that the survey process could take is estimated to be approximately two weeks due to the need to identify the groups to be surveyed and then proceed with the survey itself; with respect to data analysis it is estimated that it could take one week taking into account that the data must be digitized and then the result of the analysis obtained.

1.1.1. General Problem

What is the effect of producing software without applying a knowledge management method or tool in a computer laboratory of the San Marcos University School of Systems and Computer Engineering?

1.1.2. Specific Problems

• What is the consequence of producing software without a knowledge management tool that allows the documentation of the created software to facilitate its reuse?

• What is the consequence of producing software in a computer lab without leaving a record of the functionality and usefulness of the software created and that it can be reused?

• What is the consequence of producing software without the assistance, advice and support of people with more experience and knowledge in software development and in the need, applicability and usefulness of it?

1.2. Research Justification

When producing software in a computer laboratory, the student usually arrives alone with a previous and superficial knowledge of command syntax of some programming language provided in the best case by the person in charge of the course or having acquired knowledge on his own using the available bibliography, and in the worst case he arrives without any knowledge to experience the software production.

Software production is an activity of information search, selection of the programming language that best suits your needs, skills and interests, consultations, trial-error, doubts and exchange of information, ideas and experiences. Therefore, there is a student dynamic that is not standardized or formally established. Some knowledge management methods and tools would help students to produce software more easily and to keep the most relevant or important ones to support, sustain or continue larger and more important academic projects that are useful to the student community itself and to society in general.

1.2.1. Theoretical Justification

This study is carried out to focus on the advantages offered by knowledge management methods and tools in the production of software in a computer laboratory, establishing guidelines for group work that encourages the flow and exchange of information with which each student is imbued in order to generate new knowledge and that this new knowledge is preserved, shared and used in the best way by making use of knowledge management tools. In addition, it is sought that implicit knowledge becomes explicit and vice versa and the results of this are recorded in a history, that documentary databases are generated with the results of research and that directories of experts are created to help identify and contact the specialists in a particular subject and that all this, together with appropriate computer resources help produce specialized software and more useful.

1.2.2. Practical Justification

This study seeks to emphasize the relationship between software production and the application and use of methods and tools for knowledge management and to consider a teaching strategy so that this software produced is better shared, preserved, stored, reused and used to generate new knowledge, increasing this heritage and preserving it for future generations and in turn serve to generate the necessary or appropriate software for important projects at the academic or social level. This could help the faculty to grow technologically in the area of software development and serve as a driving force for technological development and growth at the country level.

1.2.3. Economic Justification

This can help to improve the economic heritage by reflecting in technological resources, patents and copyrights and software sales.

1.2.4. Social Justification

Software production can have a great impact on society as it would facilitate and satisfy the need of many professionals and specialized activities such as simulation, prediction, function and execution, as quoted below.

"The technology allows, through videos, demonstrations and digital simulations, to perform laboratory activities in a realistic way, but without the risks and costs associated with laboratory experiments. "" [11]. "Computer simulation is particularly useful for science learning in the following situations:

- Experiments that are very risky, expensive or time consuming.
- Delicate experiments that require precision in order for the student to appreciate patterns or trends
- Experiments that require ideal conditions, such as the absence of friction or negligible resistance

- Experiments where ethical aspects must be considered, such as experiments with live animals". [11]

"Simulation cannot completely substitute for real experimental activities, but it can help the student prepare for laboratory experiments, in the same way that simulation flights prepare the pilot before conducting real flights. One of the greatest strengths of technologies used for science education lies in the fact that they act as catalysts for change. However, used with non-traditional pedagogical models, they can significantly increase student participation and interaction, achieving their integration and involvement in learning situations. The computer today, with its multimedia features and the possibility of connecting to remote networks, rich in information of all kinds, is not only a mechanism for information management; it is, above all, a mechanism for communication and exchange. In order for the information that circulates in computers, through the networks, to be enriched and transformed into knowledge, a change in the teacher's role must be accompanied: from being a *provider of* knowledge in the classroom, to being a *mediator and facilitator of* learning within an interdisciplinary context. "" [11]

"(Waldegg, 2002) states: those who advocate the integration of NICTs for science learning claim that these technologies, developed and used appropriately, have the capacity to

- Present the materials through multiple media and channels.
- Motivate and involve students in meaningful learning activities.
- Provide graphic representations of concepts and abstract models.
- Improve critical thinking and other superior cognitive skills and processes.
- To enable the use of the information acquired to solve problems and to explain the phenomena of the environment.

- Allow access to scientific research and contact with real scientists and databases.

To offer teachers and students a platform through which they can communicate with colleagues and colleagues from distant places, exchange work, develop research and function as if there were no geographical boundaries. "

1.3. Objectives

General objective

Determine which knowledge management methods and tools are applied for the production of software in a computer laboratory of the Faculty of Systems and Computer Engineering of San Marcos University.

1.3.2. Specific Objectives

- Determine which knowledge management method teachers apply to produce software in a computer lab at the Faculty.
- Determine which knowledge management tools are applied in a computer laboratory that allows to leave record and evidence of the existence, functionality and usefulness of the software created.
- Determine which knowledge management tool is used in a computer lab that allows communication with experts in programming and with the experience and capacity necessary to guide in the creation of software.

Chapter 2. Theoretical framework

"Selecting appropriate tools for the implementation of a knowledge management project is not easy, this is due among other things, that today there is a wide variety of tools, applications, hardware, communication systems, etc. offered in the market. "" [1]

"The hard determinants of education (Trilla, 1985) collide and contrast with the new ways in which young people communicate, share, produce and learn.

Young people entering higher education today arrive with a series of practices and forms of interaction that are rarely transferred to formal learning processes. Even being immersed in a ubiquitous scenario and with a wide possession of technology, the perception and use of ICTs is framed more in an instrumental-mercantile facet (Benbenaste, 2007) than in an interiorization (Solomon, 1992) where it is configured in a facilitation for learning. "" [2]

"While students show competencies and skills that show learning that is not visible by traditional education, it is no less true that these competencies and learning are little used and perceived by subjects as facilitators for the construction of knowledge. Those who have problems with the selection of information or the preparation of materials and exams do not benefit from being Internet users; therefore, the effect of saturation and improvement of the students' possibilities by the mere use of technology does not appear as such. The fact that the students cannot represent that the use of technology is favorable for their learning strategy, is also explained by the social representation of education, located in a traditional model that is reactive to changes and anchored to static forms of time, space and transmission modes characteristic of the industrialist model. This hard core of the educational model is precisely the one that clashes with the flexibility of lifestreaming (interaction all the time), embodiment (any object connects), augmented reality and ubiquity (connection anywhere) where the digital competences of the new generations are deployed. "" [2]

"However, regardless of the level of education at which teaching takes place, the variability of the functions attributed by teachers to these technological resources is insufficient. Similarly, these resources, in most cases, are used for functions related to the transmission of information and as a resource of the educational curriculum. In relation to what has been analyzed above, in general terms, (Faustino, 2012:89) warns that the introduction of technological resources in educational institutions responds more to economic interests than to a renewal of the teaching and learning process. However, it has been observed that teachers do not experience the application of these technological tools due to the novelty of the technology and their lack of preparation for its implementation in class, hence the need for methodological preparation in this regard and measures that contribute to mitigate the deep economic limitations existing in the different centers (Marques, 2000) and (Gisbert, 2002). Consequently, if the lack of technological knowledge of professionals in society is not addressed, the impact of technologies on academic culture will be irrelevant. "" [3]

"There is a poor command of computer science, which hinders students in their search for information and argument to make value judgments. " [3]

"In this sense, the value of active learning is emphasized by the scientific literature (Beard, 2010); (Bixio, 2004), where the deficiencies in the educational formation of students due to the lack of commitment and participation within the classroom are recognized, particularly those with high student density. Despite the recognition of the importance of promoting creativity in higher education, teachers are unaware of the characteristics of learning environments that facilitate creativity. Moreover, there is a great deal of resistance and negative attitudes among students, linked to

19

personal attributes and pedagogical practices of the teacher that interact in complex ways and impact on training (Ferro+, 2010); (Felicia, 2011). "" [4]

"It may be the case, at some point, that you have students demanding to make scientific or bibliographic searches through a virtual library, and the teacher or professor does not master such technology or is not very well informed about how to operate it or the easiest thing to do, even though he or she is properly informed so that he or she can at least offer some guidance to his or her students. "" [5]

"When reviewing the available documents, it is possible to realize that the scope, complexities or importance of the use of ICTs are not detailed, so the following question arises: What do we know about ICTs in university education? When we look at the literature, we can see that authors like *Curbelo* and others agree that the greatest danger of education today is that we try to do the same as we did yesterday, with today's tools. The application and introduction of ICT as a quality indicator, integrated to the teaching and learning process in universities is complex. "" [6]

"In our society, technological changes are so numerous and occur so quickly that it is often impossible to establish new habits before the most recent ones have become established among the traditional ones. "" [7]

"As information and access to it increase exponentially, dissatisfaction with the inability of education to prepare students with the skills and knowledge necessary to function effectively in society grows (Gilbert, 1997; Mineduc, 1997; Rodriguez+, 1993). "" [8]

"(Sanchez, 2003) tells us: One of the issues of greatest concern of educational systems that have implemented technologies in schools is the curricular integration of Information and Communication Technologies, ICTs. Once the school has the technology and the teachers learn to use it, the issue that arises is how to integrate it into the curriculum. But not only that, it lacks a pedagogical method to get the most and best out of learning. In this regard, the literature on ICT curriculum integration is not entirely clear in its conceptualization and orientation. It is known in the educational arena that one of the fundamental factors that has permeated the educational use of information and communication technologies (ICTs) is the not always clear difference between the use of technologies and their curricular integration; and even less so the establishment of a knowledge management method for their better use. The difference marks a significant fact. Using technologies can imply using them for the most diverse purposes, without a clear purpose of learning from a content. "" [9]

"In Mexico, despite the fact that the university has sufficient technological infrastructure installed for the use of educational platforms, 88% of students have not used them so far, which corroborates that "Mexico shows slow progress in terms of e-learning" (Reforma, 2005). "" [10]

"The increase in access to ICTs by young university students in the metropolitan area of Mexico City is evident. Unfortunately, this access has not translated into a notable improvement in educational quality. Studies on Mexican student performance show a low level of deep learning and development of cognitive skills8 (Herrera+, 2009). "" [10]

2.1. Epistemological Framework of Information

"The word *epistemology* comes from the Greek << epistéme>>, which means <<science>> (knowledge), and from <<logos>>, which means (treatise), <<treaty of science>>. It becomes the theory, the philosophy of science. In England and Germany it is used to mean the part of logic called Criticism, or also, criteriology; therefore, <<knowing its object, extension and importance>>. It means, then, science of method and causes of knowledge, especially with reference to its limits and validity. In a broader sense, <<criticism, discussion or examination of the sciences, of their value, of their scope>>. " [50]

"Epistemology as a philosophical discipline deals with the foundations and methods of scientific knowledge. In ancient philosophy, mainly in Plato and Aristotle, there are already epistemological reflections. Some authors consider that its founder is Jhon Locke (1632-1704), who in his Essay on *Knowledge (*1690) systematically deals with the origin, essence and certainty of human knowledge; others maintain that the authentic founder of this philosophical branch is Emmanuel Kant (1724-1804), since in his *Critique of Pure Reason he* establishes the bases of scientific knowledge. "" [50]

"Epistemology becomes a reflexive mediation between scientific development and the rest of culture. "" [50]

"Master Estanislao Zuleta asks himself what it means to teach, and answers from Plato's line, as he explains in *The Sophist,* that the fundamental problem of education is to combat ignorance. Plato considers that education is not a problem similar to that of feeding a hungry person, since in this case the matter would be very simple. The real problem is to bring someone out of indigestion so that he can have an appetite. Because what prevents access to knowledge, what Plato calls <<ignorance>>, is not a lack, it is, on the contrary, an excess of opinions in which we have unfounded confidence. Prejudice, as Descartes, Spinoza or Kant called it, and which Plato called the <<opinion>>, is always present. Plato's idea, then, is that effective education has to begin by creating a need to know through the criticism of opinion. "" [50]

"Secondly, this need to know is not thought of by Plato as a need for information but as a need to think. The second criterion is to learn to think for oneself. Plato

goes so far as to say in *The Banquet* that knowledge is not transmitted from one man to another as water is transmitted from one cup to another by means of a wool wick, but that it is necessary for each one to find knowledge by his own process and to be able to give an account of what he knows by having carried out that process. That is, think for yourself your conclusions from your own premises. ""
[50]

"A line of thought on education in this direction contrasts with the effective reality of education as a workforce qualification enterprise for a market in which the qualified workforce acquires a certain cost. To the extent that this other reality imposes its demands, one will have a position completely opposite to that briefly described and synthesizing Plato's thought, according to which it is thought that develops at its own pace. How long does it take for a structure of opinions, an ideological system, to break down so that a scientific mentality can be configured on its ruins? We do not know beforehand, but there is a clear consciousness that we are forming a thinker, an investigator, a creator. "" [50]

"Then, education becomes a production of merchandise that must be subjected to the logic of the production of merchandise: minimum time, minimum cost, maximum profit; in this way it will be developed by accelerating not the formation but the information, the training, the knowledge that will be acquired in a labor market, which is increasingly specialized and restricted in terms of the field in which it must operate. Today it is possible to train then, as an example, engineers with a high level of knowledge in certain formulas, but practically illiterate in other vital fields, without the capacity to reflect on political, literary, human issues, etc. "" [50]

"According to Kant, the criteria that formative education should have are: to think for oneself, that is, the criterion of not having a passive mentality that receives its truths, and simply accepts them, from some authority, from some tradition, from

23

some prejudice; the second, the capacity to put oneself in the point of view of the other, that is, not to maintain dogmatically one's own point of view as unique and to be able to enter into dialogue with the other points of view in the perspective of bringing each one to its ultimate consequences, to establish to what extent they are coherent with oneself; and the third is to carry the already conquered truths to their last consequences, the criterion of what Kant calls *reason, that* is, to take any truth as a model to find another one, a mathematical truth or any other. "'" [50]

"There are many things that we cannot change, rhythm, time, a *pensum,* but there are others that as teachers we can improve, think about our subjects ourselves, make them restless, transmit enthusiasm, generate capacity for amazement, transmit passion for knowledge and the capacity to learn by enjoying. "'" [8]

"Scientific research is one of the most complex and important activities of the human species, in order to guarantee the viability and reproduction of the social *bios.* Science in its multiple disciplines in which it is divided, (with the purpose of covering the many problems it faces), has built from its beginnings a series of procedures that arise from deep reflection, from thought that constitutes itself as a creative force to influence reality, which is presented in the first instance as inscrutable, but that from the systematic application of these steps to know its causes and origins, becomes a space of truth for the researcher. "'" [51]

"In the search for truth, scientists and all those who were interested in science, created the methods that are guiding guides, to discover or at least get closer to know, on the one hand, the forms in which nature operates and on the other, the essence of man as a social being and his constructions. In the latter case, a series of discussions, debates, and polemics have been generated about the possible scope of the social and administrative sciences, which, at the dawn of modernity, had two disjunctions: to imitate the natural sciences or to create an identity of their own. "" [51]

2.1.1. Epistemic Traditions

"The traditions on which both the quantitative and qualitative paradigms are based have their origins in the enlightenment of the seventeenth century, with the search for rationalism, as a method of thought on which the need for man's domination over nature and man himself is built, scientific doubt and skepticism, would be the lodge of the discourse of modernity on which it would be based. In this era, instrumental reason will begin as the axis of the whole material progress of human organizations. "" [51]

"Reason now needed orderly forms of thought that would help man emancipate himself from medieval obscurantism, building the modernity and scientific advance that we are living today. But what is reason? Horkheimer and Adorno give an answer [...] reason is the instance of calculating thought that organizes the world for the purpose of self-preservation and knows no other function than that of converting the object from mere sensitive material into material of mastery. "" [51]

"The illustration that seeks in Kant's words, the liberation of man from a need for a higher level of consciousness. Enlightenment is man's exit from his minority. He himself is guilty of it. Minority lies in the inability to make use of one's own understanding, without the guidance of another. ...] *Sapere aude!* Have the courage to use your own understanding! This is the motto of the Enlightenment. Thus enlightened knowledge needs methods and techniques that take it beyond the simple perception given by its senses, but neither does it fall into a false idealism, which induces it to distort reality, that is, the method becomes a link between theory and practice that must result in truth. "" [51]

"The works of Bacon in *Novum organum* and Descartes with his work *Discourse on Method, had as their* objective to provide and promote a system of ideas and procedures logically ordered, which would be valid from explanations that were more or less objective and supported by reality, as well as by mathematics that would help to corroborate hypothetical assumptions, based on measurement, quantification and repetition of the phenomenon, thus providing the foundations for scientific research of causal explanation, which although it will be perfectly established in the natural sciences, will not be the same in the social and humanist sciences, thus having a controversy that to date continues to raise new debates, between the causal explanation (erklarën) and on the other hand the understanding (verstehen). "" [51]

"The causal explanation refers to positivist positions with respect to the ways of approaching research on social phenomena. This scientific positivism is going to try to make social, historical, economic science... following the ideal typification of mathematical physics, accentuating the relevance of the general laws for scientific explanation and trying to subsume under the same and only method all knowledge with scientific pretensions. On the other hand, a tradition will emerge that will perceive understanding as a paradigm that intends to emancipate science from mechanistic and mathematical approaches, giving a hermeneutic and less instrumental approach to scientific research that is generated in what Dilthey would call sciences of the spirit, although it is necessary to point out that: the word sciences of the spirit was introduced fundamentally with the translation of J.S. Mill's *logic*. Thus generating two traditions that would give way to what could be a false debate between the predominance of one method over another, or rather between paradigms. "" [51]

"The understanding is then a position that pretends to interpret the phenomenon from a subject-object relationship, from the recognition of social science as a product that is historically constructed and that cannot be dissociated from its producer, it is therefore a position that does not see in the measurement and in the causality the answers to human problems, considering their indivisibility and trying to know the intimate motivations of a given behavior. Understanding is a conviction based on lived evidence that is reached through lived experiences, but not demonstrable". [51]

"Thomas Kuhn when he refers to the *paradigm* expression refers in two senses:

On the one hand, it refers to the whole constellation of beliefs, values, techniques and so on, shared by the members of a given community. On the other hand, it denotes an element of that constellation, the concrete solutions to puzzles that, used as models or examples, can replace the explicit rules as a basis for the solution of the remaining puzzles of normal science. '"" [51]

"Thus understanding as a paradigm a group of beliefs that are shared in a scientific community regarding methods, techniques and ways of research, it can be said that there are a number of controversies, towards understanding how many paradigms, as well as existing methods to conduct research and which are the most appropriate, in this aspect it seems to me that there are two great traditions that have already been mentioned *erklaren* and *verstehen,* which in turn will be tied to two methodological paradigms, the quantitative and the qualitative, which will each carry a series of techniques with their own characteristics, depending on the object to be addressed, but also on the epistemological position that the researcher has or prefers. '"" [51]

"The main characteristics have already been outlined, but it is necessary to incorporate more elements and distinctive features of these methods that have been erroneously handled as antithetical, (largely because of the perception of the social and administrative sciences). We can point out that the [...] quantitative paradigm is attributed to a positivist, hypothetical-deductive, particularist, objective, results-oriented, and natural science-based view of the world. In other words, there is a strong component of elements and techniques in the measurement of these and the need for empirical verification of social facts, imitating the natural sciences. '"" [51]

"On the other hand, the qualitative paradigm (which will be more linked to understanding) will present a contrasting vision in terms of how the methodological process should be conceived. On the other hand, it is said that the qualitative paradigm is ascribed to a phenomenological, inductive, holistic, subjective, process-oriented view of the world that is proper to social anthropology. "" [51]

"In a comparison exercise, if we look at table 1, we can appreciate in detail the specific differences of both paradigms, among which it is worth noting that while one observes the phenomenon from within, the other prefers to embrace the phenomenon from outside, away from the object so as not to contaminate the research, and that is where its objectivity comes from, in contrast the qualitative paradigm recognizes its subjectivity as something inherent in the research process, pointing out the fallacy of objectivity, which is only possible when human nature is not involved. "" [51]

Table 1

Title: attributes of the qualitative and quantitative paradigms

Qualitative Paradigm	Quantitative Paradigm
It advocates the use of qualitative methods.	It advocates the use of quantitative methods.
Phenomenology and <<verstehen>>: seeks to understand human behavior from the individual's own frame of reference.	Logical-positivist: seeks the *facts or causes of* social phenomena with little attention to the subjective states of individuals.
Naturalistic and unproven observation.	Reactive and controlled measurement.
Subjective.	Objective.
Close to the data; perspective from the inside	Data section; perspective from outside.
Based on <<reality>>, discovery oriented, exploratory, expansionist, descriptive and inductive.	Not based on <<reality>>, oriented towards verification, confirmatory, reductionist, inferential and hypothetical-deductive.
Process oriented.	Result oriented.
Valid; <<real>>, <<rich>> and <deep>> data	Secure; hard and replicable data.
Not generalizable; study of isolated cases.	Generalizable, multiple case studies.
Holistic.	Particularistic.
It is a dynamic reality.	It is a stable reality.

Source. Charles Reichardt, and Thomas Cook, "Beyond Qualitative versus Quantitative Methods," in Estudios de psicología, No. 11, 1982, Spain, p. 42. Available at: http://dialnet.unirioja.es/servlet/articulo?codigo=2858142. Consultation date: 09/19/2013. (28-07-19)

"The qualitative paradigm does not pretend to present absolute truths, nor laws of general application, since it recognizes the diversity and plurality of scenarios, conditions and situations that are presented in reality, which are therefore unique and unrepeatable, so that the observations and results of its research are only valid for the particular case under study. On the other hand, the quantitative vision (due to its closeness to the natural sciences), tries to have the scope of formulating general principles, which allow it to more or less generate scenarios or tendencies that apply to the greatest number of cases. The ideal of this paradigm is to have general laws that have been obtained from mathematical calculation and objectivity, which is nothing more than rationality (inherited from the illustrated rationality), in its positive version and which gives results or products that supposedly help in the construction of the society in which we develop. "" [51]

"Now a weakness in this scheme that is rightly presented by Reichardt and Cook, has to do with the critical dimension, which is excluded from such schemes, but is necessary in both the qualitative and quantitative vision, understanding and empathy with the object of study is indispensable so that a margin of reliability can exist, but on the other hand the data without a critical perspective cannot advance, since it will not say anything transcendent for the transformation of the society in which we operate, both paradigms and methods make only a limited contribution without the critical dimension of themselves:

Neither observation nor reason constitute an authority. Intellectual intuition and imagination are very important, but are not reliable; they can show us things very clearly, and yet mislead us. They are indispensable as the main sources of our theories, but most of our theories are false anyway. The most important function of observation and reasoning, and even of intuition and imagination, is to help us in the critical examination of those bold conjectures that constitute the means by which we probe the unknown. "" [51]

"To the extent that both paradigms can construct theories or approximations for the explanation and understanding of an object of study under the critical perspective of the method they use and the result of this, one can have a minimum of certainty that such research, conjecture or theory, has a certain content of validity that can contribute to the advancement of science and the search for truth. "" [51]

"So far we can point out that there is a genealogy that follows a logic where the *weltanschauung* defines the social scientist, as to what *kind of* science he will perform from the epistemological tradition he addresses; secondly from the paradigm in which he decants and thirdly the first two conditions will lead him in a univocal way to a certain method or rather to a series of certain methods and techniques. From the traditions of understanding and explanation, the quantitative and qualitative paradigms will emerge, and from this the methods that are tied to the fundamental paradigms that we have proposed here. "" [51]

"Quantitative methods have the advantage that they can provide reliable and structured information, which allows us to weigh the reality of the problem at hand, and also that [...] they offer us the possibility of generalizing the results more widely, giving us control over the phenomena and a point of view of counting and magnitudes of these. Likewise, it offers us a great possibility of replication and a focus on specific points of such phenomena [...], of course this part includes the facility that exists to make comparisons. Likewise, the qualitative methods give us a humanist perspective, where subject and object interrelate in order to approach a particular reality without necessarily being structured, but also provides [...] depth to the data, dispersion, richness of interpretation, contextualization of the environment or setting, details and unique experiences. "" [51]

2.2. Research Background

With the introduction of ICT tools in higher education, it became necessary to reflect: How could these tools be adapted to the characteristics of each course and the different teaching methodologies and above all to the essential objective of student learning? Although the answer and implementation may be complicated, it is necessary to focus on each aspect of this puzzle to find a solution that best suits the new requirements of higher education based on the use of ICT tools. The following is a list of articles that support the background of the research:

Name of the work: The Dynamics of the Training Process for Scientific Research in Higher Education Supported by Information and Communication Technologies

Author(s): Lida de la C. Sánchez Ramírez, María Elena Pardo Gómez, José Manuel Izquierdo Lao

Date: 2010

Objectives of the research: "to develop a didactic model that, from the theoretical point of view, offers the necessary elements of how to make optimal use of all the possibilities offered by these technologies in the educational teaching process, according to the scientific research process, and which therefore constitutes the support of a didactic strategy that allows teachers to be guided in the use of these technologies in this process and thus contribute to its improvement. "

Summary of the problematic situation raised: "given the new training needs of professionals in the 21st century, universities can no longer treasure all the scientific content and much less the teachers can be reservoirs of all the information. These contents are not finished truths, but are in constant transformation, which is why it is necessary to be constantly updated. Furthermore, *interaction is necessary in the* work where time and geographical barriers are not obstacles to exchange and timely *collaboration.* "

"From diagnoses carried out in the country, research deficiencies have been evidenced in university students, during their training process in the ICT era, which is an expression of the dialectic contradiction between the possibilities between these technologies and the use of them in terms of scientific research. "

"The analysis of the possible causes of such insufficiencies led to the recognition that these technologies have not been incorporated into the training process for scientific research under a conception that scientifically bases their didactic use. "

Methodology used for the development of the work: not specific

Most important results and conclusions:

✓ "In the model of the dynamics of the formation process for scientific research, based on the ICTs, the essential relations between the configurations that characterize this process were revealed, establishing two dimensions: the innovative techno-investigative and the methodological techno-investigative, which allow to resignify the interpretation of this from a holistic and dialectical character.

✓ "The following are established as essential relations of the proposed model: from the techno-research intentionality in the development of a techno-research systematization towards the search for scientific content and the collaborative character in the construction of scientific content in the scientific research process. "

✓ "The essential regularity is given by the integrative logic that is established between the techno-investigative intentionality, the techno-investigative systematization and the collaborative construction of the scientific content, as synthesis processes in the dynamics of the formation process for scientific research, supported by the ICTs. "

Name of the work: Knowledge management of three Consolidated Academic Bodies of the Educational Area

Author(s): Juan Carlos Mijangos Noh, Karla Sugey Manzo Cabrera

Date: January-June, 2012

Research objectives: "to describe the characteristics of knowledge management carried out by consolidated academic bodies (AC) in the area of education, in order to recognize patterns that allow the consolidation of other ACs in the educational area".

Synthesis of the problematic situation raised: "the evidence collected in the case of the three CAs participating in this study shows that the process of these towards consolidation has not been free of problems related to their respective processes of knowledge management, which we can classify in the following areas:

Problems associated with the contradictions between the forms of knowledge management that existed in the moments prior to the establishment of the policies of the Promep, the regulated institutional framework that marks the creation and development of the ACs.

Problems related to strategic decision making about the valorization of ACs. According to the focus group and interviews conducted, these problems arise from the fact that the Promep came to institute not only rules, but also new roles linked to the participation and management of AAs. We have evidence that in all cases AAs, in particular coordinators and members of the core group, interact sometimes in contradiction and sometimes frankly in conflict with agents from instances established within universities before the emergence of AAs. "

Methodology used for the development of the work: "group interviews, individual interviews, written response to open questions. "

Most important results and conclusions: "The results of the study confirm what they propose (Rodriguez, 2006) and (Fainholc, 2006), about the need to establish the framework of rules and standards in which knowledge management is developed. We can say that, in addition to the discipline and skill with which knowledge management should be directed and operated in order to favorably condition the catalysis of the achievement of objectives, it is also important to consider the type of members of each group. The correct recognition and use of the disciplinary diversity gives a guideline for a better adaptation to teamwork and allows to obtain greater benefits. In this case, the benefit of the very diverse disciplinary backgrounds of the studied CA members has had a remarkable role in knowledge management processes. Finally, we propose the need that, from the findings obtained in this study, new researches are made in order to identify more characteristics about the micro processes that are developed in each CA and to be able to describe the internal dynamics of the groups. Perhaps the particularities of such dynamics also condition knowledge management. Likewise, we recommend the study of the links between the type of leadership and knowledge management, since in our research we find some elements that allow us to glimpse an important relationship between these two components of the life of the ACs. "

Name of the work: "Knowledge Management in the New Cuban University".

Authors: "Dr. Vivian Estrada Sentí, Dr. Francisco Benítez Cárdenas

Date: 2006

Research objectives: "to universalize knowledge and achieve a comprehensive general culture for our citizens, to analyze the development of knowledge management in universities and the strategies that make possible its improvement both in the international and Cuban context, in order to consolidate the transformations towards a new university. "

Summary of the problematic situation: "the vertiginous development of technology, produced fundamentally from the second half of the 20th century and its immediate assimilation in some countries, has favored the creation of conditions for the transition from societies based on tangible production to societies where the fundamental feature is the production of knowledge and intangibles, whose value sometimes exceeds that of the material production itself. In this way, the concept has been coined that we are in the presence of knowledge-based societies.

While this may be true for a few countries, the majority of the world's population continues to be economically and socially backward, and the gap between developed countries and the rest of the planet is widening, accentuating inequalities both between the countries themselves and within the social strata of the so-called developing countries.

It is a reality that those developing countries that want to take advantage of the opportunities provided by this new paradigm must develop aggressive policies in the field of education. "

Methodology used for the development of the work: not specific.

Most important results and conclusions: "Universities have always been institutions totally focused on knowledge and its <u>management, therefore, it is </u>an opportunity and a necessity in their high educational responsibility and in the preparation of scenarios to apply the methods and techniques appropriate to the context and objectives of the organizations. The different processes that use and generate information in universities and that are basic to reach knowledge must be specially attended to individually and in their integration, storage, transfer, use and evaluation of this knowledge and its interrelations. "

"In particular, the teaching and learning process should benefit from the changes that the introduction of ICTs allows today, but this is conditioned to the development of effective actions in its organization and planning, as well as in the preparation of teachers. "

Name of the work: Model for the Development of Knowledge Management in the Research Centers of the Colombian Public Universities Application case Pedagogical and Technological University of Colombia (UPTC)

Author(s): José Javier Gonzales Millán

Date: 2009

Research objectives: "to generate environments that encourage the optimal application and development of knowledge management in the university. To make a brief theoretical conceptualization referring to the subject of knowledge management, to present its applications and its current state in higher education, specifically in the research centers of the Universidad Pedagógica y Tecnológica de Colombia (UPTC), to determine guidelines for the development of its management and to present a theoretical model for the optimal performance of knowledge management in the public university, making some allusions to the Colombian university. "

Synthesis of the problematic situation raised: "the fundamental reason why research is carried out on this object is due to the organic research conformation of the UPTC, which heads the research direction (Din)[1] , an organ assigned to the academic vice-rectory of the institution. This is subdivided into research centers, which are nothing more than a figure of administrative management and operational procedures. Based on this clarity, it is necessary to focus on the groups that make up each research center, because that is where the products and other variables related to knowledge management are found, unlike centers in which there is no activity of any kind that is typical of research knowledge management processes, much less references to categorization or productivity related to Colciencias standards. "

Methodology used for the development of the work: "in this article we used descriptive research. Researchers who are experts in the field, such as the directors of the research groups, were consulted. A survey was conducted among those responsible for implementing research and knowledge management policies at UPTC. The attached survey was used as an instrument for self-diagnosis of knowledge management in research groups at the Universidad Pedagógica y Tecnológica de Colombia. Databases, journals, documents and reports were consulted and documents were retrieved. "

Most important results and conclusions:

• "It is necessary to introduce flexibility in university organizations in Latin America and Colombia to adequately face the fast pace of technological development and other transformations of the contemporary world. "

• "The research centers have high quality human capital, but the incentives are low and the conditions of access to technology are limited, due to the budget allocated by the nation and by Colciencias. "

• "The knowledge management processes in research centers present shortcomings that do not allow rapid progress in scale and recognition in Colciencias; likewise, opportunities are lost to access the resources that this entity offers to researchers. "

• "In relation to qualitative factors, productivity stands out, reaching an average of 4.65 products per researcher; as for economic support, it is rather deficient. The Internet is a tool of great use for the transference of knowledge; on the other hand, it was demonstrated that the groups have, in their majority, a trajectory superior to seven years. The average number of members is 26; due to their degree of involvement, permanent teachers, temporary teachers and young researchers stand out. "

• "The study, in its final part, revealed that, in the time of existence and the members, specifically the plant teachers and young researchers, are those who best help to generate knowledge. The research groups have high quality human capital,

38

but the stimulus is low and the conditions of access to technology are limited, as well as the reception of economic incentives; on the other hand, a process of processing is detected for the establishment of research, which affects its efficiency and allows to classify, in general, the UPTC in a medium range of research knowledge management. Finally, the research presented a theoretical model and proposals for the development and consolidation of knowledge management in the university groups, oriented towards continuous improvement and the creation of guidelines that allow it to be clearly identified. "

Name of the work: "Digital Access Gap Between University Professors, according to their Discipline. "

Author(s): "Ana Teresa Morales Rodríguez and Alberto Ramírez Martinell"

Date: May 2015

Research objectives: "to determine the existing differences between university professors of four careers in ICT. "

Summary of the problematic situation raised: "the digital divide is a phenomenon that occurs in the context of the Information and Communication Society (Castells, 2002) and refers to the inequalities that exist with respect to the use of technology (Crovi, 2009). It should be noted that the *Digital Divide is* not a static, completely limited, or universal concept, but rather a phenomenon of multiple dimensions, which allows us to identify different types of gaps among which we can mention the cognitive; the use; the appropriation; the generational; and the access to mention a few (Ramirez+, 2013). The access gap is characterized by the technological infrastructure conditions of a nation, a group of people or an individual. In the case of this study, the possible digital gap between groups of teachers from four different academic disciplines is analyzed. "

Methodology used for the development of the work: "the methodology used for this study, part of the Digital Divide project3 , in which a survey instrument was developed based on international ICT standards, from international organizations such as OECD, ISTE, UNESCO, ILCE and ACRL. This instrument consists of various sections that delve into the technological appropriation of university teachers, among which we find: Socioeconomic level; perception about ICT; digital knowledge of a computer type such as device management, files, text and rich text management, multimedia content management, among others; and informational knowledge such as literacy and digital citizenship of university teachers. For this article, we use the section of general information and the socioeconomic one, since the latter gives information about the digital devices that the professor has, and his degree of connectivity to the Internet. "

"The application of the instrument was carried out in each of the four faculties that make up this study, in the case of the first three the application was done in the framework of the Digital Knowledge Workshop of the Digital Divide Project, where information was also extracted that contributes to the knowledge of the current situation - of ICT infrastructure - of the academic entities in which the teachers work; and in the case of the computer science teachers the application of the same instrument was done by ten interviewers who personally addressed the teachers to ask for their support in answering the survey. The universe of the population is constituted by 186 teachers and 108 were surveyed, distributed as follows: 10 out of 24 philosophy teachers; 35 out of 64 English language teachers; 15 out of 36 biology teachers; and 48 out of 62 computer science teachers. There were a total of 186 teachers, of which 108 answered the survey. "

Most important results and conclusions: "This article explored access to ICTs, understood as the provision of computers; access to internet and mobile devices (Smartphone and tablet), to make a comparison of the access that teachers of four disciplines have, to discover that in terms of computer and connectivity there are no significant differences between the four academic communities studied, thus rejecting the hypothesis of the existence of a digital access gap, since 100% of all the teachers in this study have one or more computers -either desktop or portable-, they access the internet practically all the time since they remain connected in their respective work entities, at home, and there are even teachers who have complementary mobile devices with internet connection. "

"However, there are tonalities in the access to ICTs, according to the nature of the teachers' disciplines, and among the most important we can mention that in all the degrees there is a tendency to prefer the laptop, highlighting that the hard disciplines have a greater number of teachers who have one and it is in them where the low preference of the desktop computer is denoted; about where the teachers obtain the technological resources, an advantage of the hard disciplines over the soft ones is revealed, since given their scientific, empirical and practical character they have greater opportunity to generate products that are translated into economic benefits coming from recognitions such as PEDPA, PROMEP and SIN; and with respect to mobility, the general panorama is not encouraging, since in terms of connectivity there is no faculty in which the number of teachers with a Smartphone data plan exceeds 44%, and the applied disciplines have a greater number of teachers who have access to mobile connectivity, and this coincides with the low level of access to mobile devices such as Smartphones and tablets, where again differences in access were found, which allows us to reflect on the indispensability of these devices according to the needs of each discipline. In some of the elements analyzed, an advantage of hard disciplines became evident in the case of obtaining ICT resources, and in other cases of those applied in the possession of mobile devices and connectivity. "

"In summary, the computer and Internet connection are basic for teachers of any discipline, and in terms of devices and mobile connectivity there are differences according to the uses that may have the devices and how significant it may be for the purposes of each field of knowledge. "

"Finally, it is recognized that teachers have overcome the access gap, however, it is necessary -and also the next stage of this research- to study the skills they have for their management, the frequency of use of these technologies and the intentionality or purposes for which they use them, and thus be able to differentiate the degree of use, and appropriation of ICTs, according to the discipline of the teachers. "

2.3. Theoretical Basis

2.3.1. Theoretical References

"Knowledge as a concept has been treated from different perspectives, for example, Polanyi (1966) states that human beings have knowledge that is often difficult to transfer; within the organization there can also be explicit knowledge that can be transferred with the help of rules, procedures, mathematical expressions, among others. There are also some visions that speak of knowledge as a result of the elaboration of each person from the information they possess through the application of learning processes (Quintanilla, 2003; Serban and Luan, 2002). ""
[7]

"Maturana and Varela (1984) define knowledge as the cognitive beliefs, confirmed, experienced and contextualized of the knower about the object, which will be conditioned by the environment and will be enhanced and systematized by the knower's capabilities, which establish the basis for objective action and value generation. Often in organizations it is not only rooted in documents or databases, but also in institutional routines, processes, practices and norms. "" [7]

"On the other hand, Benavides and Quintana (2005) state that knowledge management helps organizations to make decisions to solve problems based on a method that rescues four variables: identification and measurement, generation, capture and storage, access and transfer. On the other hand, we find authors like Bhatt (2001) who focus on knowledge management as a result of the formation of social and technological subsystems within the organization that in turn help in the formation of organizational competencies. Others like Kogut and Zander (1992) focus on the growth of knowledge within the organization and are among the first to highlight its strategic importance within the organization. "'" [7]

"We must bear in mind that to speak about the theory of knowledge creation, two dimensions must be taken into account, the ontogenetic and the epistemological; the first one speaks about the environment in which knowledge is generated, it depends on the individual and how it expands in an organized way. The second is based on the process of communication around conversational modes based on tacit and explicit knowledge. "'" [7]

2.3.2. Knowledge Management

ESTRADA, Vivian (2006) states: "The dizzying development of technology, produced fundamentally from the second half of the 20th century and its immediate assimilation in some countries, has favored the creation of conditions for the transition from societies based on tangible production to societies where the fundamental feature is the production of knowledge and intangibles, whose value sometimes exceeds that of the material production itself. In this way, the concept has been coined that we are in the presence of knowledge-based societies. "'" [12]

"It is a reality that those developing countries that want to take advantage of the opportunities provided by this new paradigm must develop aggressive policies in the field of education. "'" [12]

Development

"Knowledge management does not emerge as an isolated idea, it is by its own characteristics a set of actions inherent in human activity, it is a process, so it can be studied, organized, structured and applied creatively in an organization. "" [12]

"There has been an increasing demand for continuous training by professionals, mainly due to the current speed of knowledge creation and transfer. Knowledge Management is an appropriate discipline to attend and integrate fluently the new needs of higher education, both in the management of the university institution itself and in its research and teaching functions. "" [12]

"In the case of universities, and in view of the new needs caused by the current economic, social and technological context, the application of knowledge management must be directed both at the internal reorganization of processes, and at the improvement of teaching and research, with the aim of facilitating the development of a competitive university adapted to the new demands of society. "" [12]

"The main mission of Knowledge Management is to create an environment in which the knowledge and information available in an organization is accessible and can be used to stimulate innovation and improve decision making. The key is to create a culture in which information and knowledge are valued, shared, managed and used effectively and efficiently. "" [12]

"Despite the years that have passed in the so-called knowledge society, it happens that much of the information that passes through the universities continues to be in paper format and when some process is automated, it is still, in a good part of the cases, the classic ones and with isolated treatment. Universities have always been institutions totally focused on knowledge and its management, therefore, it is an opportunity and a necessity in its high educational responsibility and in the preparation of scenarios to apply the methods and techniques appropriate to the context and objectives of the organization. It is very important to identify the processes that use and generate information in universities and that are basic to achieve knowledge. "" [12]

"Knowledge management is a set of strategies and processes to identify, capture and socialize knowledge in order to help the organization be more competitive. "" [12]

"Learning is not simply the acquisition of information, it is improving our ability to initiate action and achieve sustained improvement in performance and the way in which the organization understands and facilitates learning and innovation, the way in which it encourages workers to transmit and receive knowledge. Enhancing the information resources generated by each organization, analyzing its flows, managing them effectively has become an unavoidable necessity. "" [12]

"Among the main aspects to be addressed, as part of a strategy for Knowledge Management, we can highlight

- **The creation of knowledge communities** by related branches of knowledge and transdisciplinary that guarantee the necessary human relationship to achieve an effective flow of knowledge (in universities all the conditions exist for this, but it is necessary to act consciously in this sense).
- To **have an** efficient **intranet for the exchange of** information, knowledge and experiences
- **Systematic updating of the information** needed to make decision making faster and more effective.
- To **have databases that** benefit students, professors and researchers (digitalization of all internal documents necessary for the development of study and research, documents of professors and researchers, student papers, exams from

45

previous courses, etc.) all of which can be organized with the use of tools for this purpose such as concept maps.

• **Manage tacit knowledge and convert it into explicit knowledge** (whenever possible) and find methodologically adequate ways to present it in teaching materials (articles, books, theses, monographs, etc.), organizational materials, regulations and others that contribute to maintain and improve its intellectual capital.

• To **have a repository of information** - of knowledge - to which all workers have access, complemented with communication tools to exchange experiences, knowledge and case studies, which will imply an improvement in the management processes. "" [12]

"It should be noted that given two basic conditions: technological development and cultural change, much of what happens with regard to Knowledge Management is the exploration of new management models of the organization taking into account the technological or computer element, but in essence expresses a new way of relating to information and knowledge where it is not enough to have access to large amounts of information, it is necessary that individuals can and know how to process it. "" [12]

"Generally, much more time is spent on the search for information than on its analysis, the latter being the most important. It is useless for an organization to have individuals with talent and knowledge, if that knowledge is not taken advantage of by this organization. "" [12]

"While it is true that in practice very few organizations are applying and developing Knowledge Management fully, mainly due to the complexity of its treatment and the fact that there are no professionals fully trained to act as guides in such processes, this does not diminish its importance and significance mainly in combination with ICT and the use of appropriate tools for this purpose. "" [12]

"Educational institutions must assume the management of knowledge and insert themselves in the information society by assuming a leadership position. Carrying out a program of knowledge management in the educational sphere can be said to be indispensable for at least the following reasons

1.   To achieve higher quality face-to-face, blended and distance learning, not only because of what this means for students, but also for teachers.

2.   The existing need to cover new skills and competences of students and professionals.

3.   The growing generation of information in digital format, as well as procedures and tools for its processing.

4.   The need to develop specific strategies for the new university that will facilitate learning and gain in effectiveness and efficiency "" [12]

"At this stage we are living it is not enough to have access or possess information, it is necessary to know how to make an adequate use of it in the resolution of problems or real situations. That is to say, to have the capacity to transform and transfer that initial information into knowledge within very concrete spaces of time and situations. It is in this point where there is a special interest. "" [12]

"Situated from the perspective of the Knowledge Society, some of the issues to be addressed and strengthened are

•   **Development and improvement of blended and distance education,** as these become an essential model in the conception of the new university.

•   **manage and organize the basic knowledge for different courses in** a way that facilitates their access using appropriate tools such as concept maps. Working with digital databases and telematic networks.

•   **Development of new content and values** (collaborative work, computer applications, etc.)

- **Use of pedagogical strategies** that favour learning, compatible with knowledge management such as problem-based learning, etc.
- To **strengthen and prioritize the role of the tutor,** not only as the traditional academic figure in universities, but in his role as educator and mentor, who is capable of transmitting and creating values in students to ensure, along with the experiential environment of this, their comprehensive training as citizens and future professionals. "" [12]

"ICTs and the Internet in particular, together with the ever closer generalization of knowledge bases, are the new area of research, development and services for information professionals. If, on the one hand, ICTs mean the elimination of many of the barriers to access to information, there are two basic issues that have to be very present in the educational issue and the acquisition of new knowledge, they are

- The information available must be organized and of good quality.
- To have quality computer resources to improve the management of the necessary contents. "" [12]

"That is to say, we cannot say that by itself the Web or information in digital media are an adequate resource for training, so it requires computer tools that help to facilitate the management of content. "" [12]

"In blended **and distance learning, in** particular, the quality of information within the digital media then becomes a factor with enormous implications for the creation and transfer of knowledge. "" [12]

"In addition to its traditional use, for the purposes of knowledge management, special attention should be paid to the effect that technologies produce in the way we communicate, research, study, prepare classes, because these **are indicators**

that are difficult to measure, but of relevant importance. It is no longer only the computer as a teaching medium that is to be examined, but whether it is networked, which network it is connected to, which knowledge base it is accessed by, what applications it has, etc. For universities there are two key aspects linked to knowledge management, which in turn are directly interrelated:

a)   The creation of favorable conditions in the university scenario.

b)   The training of knowledge managers for the future, equipped with the appropriate values. "" [12]

"The profound and rapid transformations that technological development imprints on today's world have repercussions on the model of the professional. New demands appear both for the professional who is to be trained in today's university classrooms, both in person and for graduated and practicing professionals who participate in continuing education, throughout their lives. "" [12]

"BALMORI, Rocío (2012) states; management is making things happen in any area of knowledge; however, when we say knowledge management we are talking about creation, transfer, storage, application and use of knowledge itself; what must be considered is a very important element: intellectual capital. In any area of knowledge, and even more so in education, intellectual capital is involved. "13] "Unfortunately, until very recently, there was concern in higher education about knowledge management; few higher education institutions (HEIs) have managed to take advantage of the richness of this type of management, when it is in higher education that knowledge is or should be gestated. "" [13]

"We are human and one of our characteristics is that we are routine. In each new course we teach the knowledge we consider necessary for the subject we are presenting. We are not yet in the habit of sharing the subject with our students. We continue to impart the knowledge. It is here where a greater knowledge could be gestated, since all the students bring with them certain knowledge about the subject we are dealing with. Thus, we could build in each class, with new students, new knowledge based on the one developed in the last class between the teacher and the students. This is a way to promote what is knowledge management in the IES. ""' [13]

"López, G. (2005) states: knowledge management has greater relevance in institutions that are born and develop historically for that purpose: universities. From the point of view of the management of these institutions, especially those in Latin America, the time seems to be coming to implement explicit and specific systems to manage and value the knowledge they possess. ""' [14]

Knowledge Management

"Given the growing weight of intellectual capital in companies in today's world, its management acquires particular relevance, and by virtue of its association with the process of creating and managing knowledge, the expressions intellectual capital management or knowledge management are often used interchangeably. Due to this, it can be said that knowledge management is the set of processes and systems that lead to increase intellectual capital in an organization. ""' [14]

University

"The university is a knowledge-based organization whose mission, with different emphases depending on the university, is to generate or create, transmit and disseminate knowledge. The generation or creation of knowledge is usually associated with the research function; the transmission of knowledge to the teaching function; and the diffusion or dissemination of knowledge to the extension function. As a knowledge-intensive organization, its capacity to manage the creation, transmission, and dissemination of knowledge becomes crucial in the contemporary world. ""' [14]

Universities and knowledge management

"The valorization of knowledge, of growing relevance, is a component of management that companies must carry out and for which they definitely do not seem to be adequately prepared. Recent studies (Jensen and Thursby (2001)), show that universities have not been able to value, commercialize, negotiate and even allocate resources to the production of knowledge, especially in the case of those that have a medium to short term commercial orientation and there are numerous difficulties that universities face when they try to value activities whose results have uncertain benefits or in terms that are difficult to estimate or whose pricing is not conventional in market economies. In the particular case of the university, whose raison d'être is the creation, transmission and dissemination of knowledge, the valorization of the activities developed within it has multiple complexities of appropriation from the institutional point of view and from the point of view of the community that hosts it. "" [14]

"Until recently, the creation of knowledge was recognized as a process almost exclusive to research centers and universities. However, in the last decade, with the boom that has taken the intellectual capital as one of the intangible resources that gives greater value to companies, business management theories have turned on knowledge management, resulting in proposals for models on creation, storage and distribution of knowledge. Paradoxically, little has been explored about the applicability of these models in universities whose main business is precisely knowledge management. "" [14]

"MEJÍA, Mónica (2013) states: in today's organizations, possessing knowledge is not enough, because first they must make sure that it is the necessary one to carry out the tasks, as well as that it is accessible to the people who require it and that it can be stored, transmitted and used in their processes. "" [15]

"The process of Knowledge Management, includes more than the adequate use of information technologies, it implies the trust and cooperation of the people involved in the organization, who share an organizational vision and who work in an organizational environment that promotes organizational learning with the conversion of tacit to explicit knowledge. "" [15]

CASAS, Miguel (2005) states: "in any society, whether it is developed or developing, the key factor for its progress is its effective capacity to generate, and continuously apply Knowledge to the various fields of social, technical and scientific life. Consequently, the main and essential instrument for the complex processes of transformation and modernization of these societies is education, and within it, especially the university. But it is not about education and the university in its usual and traditional forms, but about a whole rethinking of new forms of organization, administration, research and action. These changes can be driven by innovative theories and processes enabled by new information and communication technologies. "" [16]

University and the Knowledge Society

"In a world like the present one, characterized by an incessant and unexpected change, and by a growing Globalization, the classic paradigm of a traditional and almost immutable university is not very congruent with the new social and scientific realities and demands, both present and future. On the other hand, if we consider that, increasingly, important research agrees that no current society is superior to its universities, it is clear that an essential instrument of progress and development is the university. In fact, there are no truly advanced countries that do not have an efficient university system and, within it, solid and permanent research. These statements are particularly important in the case of Latin America, since even some of its most outstanding universities are currently showing serious and continuous limitations in order to quickly and profoundly modify their obsolete models, structures and procedures, so as to be able to respond functionally and opportunely to new and demanding demands. "" [16]

"According to Mijangos, J. C. and Manzo, K. S. (January-June, 2012) a critical examination of the concept of knowledge management is: Knowledge has become an indispensable element for economic and social development due to the importance it has acquired as a new production factor, since it is the basis for actions derived from the combination of information, experiences, values and internal norms (Rodriguez, 2006; Davenport & Prusak, 2001, cited in Romero, 2007). "" [28]

"PÁEZ, Meivys (2012) states: pedagogical knowledge in Higher Education is constituted by the organized set of data, information, experience and know-how in the pedagogical field, this impacts directly in the formative processes through the transformations and decision making in the formation of professionals and pedagogical improvement of the teachers. However, the new challenges that are presented today in Higher Education lead to rethinking the ways in which this knowledge is managed in universities. "" [17]

"Organizational learning is more than the sum of the parts of individual learning (Dodgson, 1995). An organization does not lose its learned capabilities when members leave the organization. Organizational learning contributes to the organization's memory. Thus, learning systems not only influence current members, but also future members, due to the accumulation of stories, experiences and norms. "" [17]

"GONZALES, José (2009) states: knowledge management is nowadays an element of great importance for organizational development and, before being a means of development, it becomes an end, that is why it is valued in the academic field as one of the elements of the university's work, especially regarding research and research centers, in such a way that this item is among the three fundamental pillars of the university mission. For this reason, it is of great importance to generate environments that promote the optimal application and development of knowledge management in the university. ""' [18]

Conceptualization of knowledge management

"It is pertinent to quote, in the first instance, Drucker (1993:87), who highlights the value of knowledge as an asset, important for organizations. He shows that it is the most relevant resource in a company, so today efforts are made to define how to acquire, retain and manage it. ""' [18]

"Karl Sbeiby (1997) describes knowledge management by means of two aspects related to the line of influence, which, originally, go from an engineering to a humanistic vision. From this point of view, personnel management and information management are identified. Going a little deeper into its theory, there is a third current, focused on the process of knowledge management in the organization; for this reason, the three currents related to the subject must be known, as described below. ""' [18]

Perspective of information

"It highlights knowledge management as a cycle of administration and treatment of information, so that it is recreated within the organization, through assimilation and capture mechanisms to present practical solutions and generate new knowledge. ""' [18]

"Pavez (2001:21) states that knowledge management "embodies the organizational process that seeks the synergistic combination of data and information processing, through the capabilities of information technologies and human creativity and innovation. ""' [18]

"Based on these assessments, it is established that information related to information technology is closely linked to knowledge management, which makes this a mechanism to develop technological innovations. This is demonstrated in Western philosophy, which focuses its information on structure, while Eastern organizations are inclined to the conception of knowledge evidenced in people; that is, it is represented in human action. "" [18]

Process perspective

"In this current are authors like Quintas (Zorrilla, 1997: 2), who defines it as the process of continuously managing knowledge of all kinds to meet present and future needs, to identify and exploit knowledge resources in order to achieve organizational objectives. Also Macintosh (Zorrilla, 1997: 2) and Clemmons (2002: 9) concept it as a systematic process of the organization to achieve success through the creation, capture and sharing of knowledge. In the same way, Garcia (2002: 2) presents a cyclical definition expressed as a process of explicitly managing non-material assets and exists so that the company can generate, search, store and transfer knowledge and thus achieve increased productivity and competitiveness. In support of the above, authors such as Shanhong (2002:2) and Rodriguez (2001:13-30) support the concept of knowledge management, based on the cycle of planning, organizing, coordinating and controlling the various activities that lead to the creation and dissemination of knowledge efficiently in the company or any other type of organization. "" [18]

"It can be concluded that knowledge management obeys a logical cycle that, in general terms, begins with the identification, creation, capture, sharing, storage and transfer of knowledge, whether tacit or explicit. This generates competitiveness and efficiency in the organizations, that is, the corporate objectives are achieved. "" [18]

Humanistic perspective

"It is based on intellectual capital (IC) as a differentiating element within a process of managing knowledge flows, generated in organizations and related to value systems. This point embodies the direction of the human effort of the organization, which promotes progress between phases of the knowledge cycle. Authors such as Sbeiby (1997) and Serradell and others (2000:5), state that the management of intellectual capital in an organization has the purpose of adding value to the products and services offered by the organization in the market and to differentiate them competitively. Garrido (2002), Grau (2001:3) and Saint-Onge (Pavez, 2001:1-31) reinforce the concept, based on the ability to develop, maintain, influence and renew intangible assets, also called intellectual capital. Additionally, Arbonies (Arbonies 2006: 4-15) considers knowledge management as a set of management disciplines that treats intellectual capital as an asset of the company; therefore, it requires technological tools and mechanisms that allow for the overcoming of barriers that prevent the sharing of knowledge in order to achieve specific business objectives. "" [18]

"A review of the common elements of the definitions of creation, capture, use, dissemination, differentiation and influence of knowledge, leads to this work to consider knowledge management as: the process of creation, capture, distribution, sharing, assimilation, exploitation, use and renewal of knowledge as an element generating added value in organizations to make them more competitive, using human capital. The above has allowed us to establish a definition of knowledge management that fits the process of university research. "" [18]

"TORRES, Karla (2015) states: Today, knowledge and information are considered vital resources for organizations, so some of them have realized that the creation, transfer and management of knowledge are essential for success. "" [19]

Introduction

"Information management is decisive both for excellence and competitiveness in companies and for the quality of decision making in organizations for the social and cultural development of people; this management has become increasingly complex due to the explosion of supply and demand for information and the development of information and communication technology in the field of telematics during the twenty-first century; this is why there must be changes in organizations so that knowledge is involved in each of its members. "" [19]

Knowledge Management

"It is a process that supports organizations in finding relevant information, selecting, organizing and communicating it to all active staff; this cycle is necessary for actions such as problem solving, energizing learning and decision making. Knowledge management can improve the performance of the organization on the way to achieving an intelligent organization, but it is not enough by itself; since it involves planning strategies and establishing policies and also the collaboration of all staff of the organization a high sense of commitment to perform their work and acceptance of the process.

Bueno (1999) defines it as the function that plans, coordinates and controls the flows of knowledge that occur in the company in relation to its activities and its environment in order to create essential competencies. According to Reaich, Gemino and Sauer (2012), knowledge management should foster a social and technological environment that favors knowledge-related activities, in order to promote the creation, storage and dissemination of knowledge. For Figuerola (2013) it is the practice of organizing, storing and sharing vital information, so that everyone can benefit from its use. That is, it is seen as a set of techniques and tools involved in the process of storing, distributing, sharing and communicating data and information, in order to improve communications and knowledge among employees of an organization, allowing continuous learning, through past

experiences or lessons learned, which have been previously captured and stored. ""
[19]

"Therefore, a knowledge-based organization implies a general search for traditional management approaches, but with a new business approach that manages to combine information systems with human resource capabilities (participation, commitment, motivation and responsibility of workers) to achieve organizational objectives. "" [19]

"ESCOBAR, Ruth (2013) tells us: the integration of e-learning tools in knowledge management facilitates the processes of capture, organization, storage and transfer of information, to later access and manage it. "" [49]

Knowledge Management
"To understand the topic of knowledge management, the following definition is presented: Knowledge management emphasizes facilitating and managing activities related to knowledge such as creation, capture, transformation and use. Its function is to plan, implement, operate and manage all knowledge-related activities and programs required for the effective management of intellectual capital". [49]

The quotes [7, 33, 23] "support the different stages of which the knowledge management process is composed. These begin with the location of available internal and external knowledge; then the explicit knowledge that will be stored and made available to those who need it is identified among the sources of knowledge, and the tacit knowledge will be represented on a location map to identify the people who possess it; later, in the knowledge creation stage, the explicit knowledge will be extracted to be combined and to generate new knowledge; finally, the most important phase of the whole cycle consists of assimilating and using the created and stored knowledge. "

DEL SAZ, Miguel Angel (2000) states: "Knowledge management represents a new trend in the way a company or organization operates and manages. Its implementation has factors that are favorable (pros) to be carried out and also with other unfavorable (cons), both human and organizational. Knowledge management (KM) is a new methodology, organizational scheme and operating process that aims to apply to the world of business or any type of social organization (state entity, non-profit society, etc.). In it, <u>knowledge is</u> seen as a <u>critical resource</u> that must be managed effectively to contribute to greater social and/or economic profitability of the company and other vital objectives for its survival: customer satisfaction, growth or expansion in the market, better presentation and quality of products and services, optimization of performance and satisfaction of internal staff. ''" [21]

Knowledge management

"Through knowledge management, the aim is to identify, organize and rationally exploit explicit knowledge (that which is registered, or susceptible of being registered, by the organization) and to transform the greatest possible amount of tacit knowledge (that possessed by the individuals of the company) into explicit knowledge. It implies a strong change in the traditional company's scheme and must be done in a gradual, rational way and avoiding imbalances. These will be originated as a consequence of the push of the innovative forces, favorable to the change, and of the resistance or opposition of the immobilists, in consonance with the principle of action and reaction of physics, and giving place to attitudes of dynamic type and of static immobilism, so much to individual level as collective. Both very rapid change (strong growth with disorder) and inertia (slow reflex movement without real growth) should be avoided. ''" [21]

"As noted, its implementation should be done gradually, making staff aware that initially it will be partial, and then in phases of low intensity and controlled, choosing pilot experiences in certain areas of the organization. A sudden and intense transformation will be avoided, because it can produce a surprise effect and provoke negative reactions that, finally, can lead to the project not being successful. "" [21]

"QA implies an effective use of knowledge, in a continuous and endless way, that is to say, with a constant evolution, and has 4 objectives (**Davenport**):" [21]

1.   "Create knowledge deposits, of which there are three types: external knowledge (for example, competitive intelligence), internal knowledge (reports) and informal internal or tacit knowledge (capturing tricks, experiences, intuitions, etc., in a computer support). "" [21]

2.   "Optimize access to knowledge. Finding the person with the knowledge you need and successfully transferring it to another is a difficult process (network and expert database management). Sometimes, it can be convenient to simply facilitate the exchange of tacit knowledge rather than making a deposit, using communication tools such as video conferencing, communication networks..." [21]

3.   "Improve the knowledge environment. Make its creation, transfer and sharing more effective; change behavior about it and create a cultural receptivity to this type of functioning. "" [21]

4.   "Manage it as an asset. Some companies are focused on managing specific knowledge-intensive assets to increase their profits or income (e.g., managing their own patents, licensing patents for profit). It is better to manage assets than to measure them, because measurement requires accounting changes. "" [21]

"The most common type of QA success involves operational improvements limited to a particular process or function. Typical projects have been aimed at improving new products, supporting customers, conducting education and training missions, studying software developments, and managing patents more effectively (**Davenport**). "" [21]

2.3.3. Intellectual Capital

CARABALLO, Yeter (2009) comments: "following the line of Salazar del Castillo (2004), one gets to know the importance of carrying out a quantification, at least approximate, of the knowledge generated in companies or intellectual capital. This term emerged in the early nineties in the United States and Sweden, and measures the value of the company's knowledge in its various fields: people (human intelligence), the organization (the company's know-how[1], patents and trademarks) and the market (customer satisfaction). However, measuring intellectual capital is interesting, especially if it incorporates the commitment to make it grow, hence it was immediately associated with another term, knowledge management - knowledge management-. Nonaka and Takeuchi (1995) propose to do so through four modes of knowledge conversion: socialization, externalization, combination and internalization. ""' [22]

"The combination of the four modes of knowledge conversion proposed by Nonaka and Takeuchi (1995), together with the scenario where knowledge moves in the organization (Bosch 2002), are factors that, in our opinion, play a fundamental role in the identification, creation and transfer of knowledge. ""' [22]

"In the 90's, it is in this scenario where the concept of knowledge management appears, understood as the process of capturing the collective expertise of an organization, (company or institution), and its availability to improve the transfer and circulation, while allowing innovation. Its objective is to take advantage of the accumulated intellectual work, even if it has been done for other developments (Bosch 2002). In relation to the people -holders of the tacit knowledge- of the organization, D' Alos-Moner (2003) states that managing an institution today is largely a matter of managing these 'knowledge workers'. For this, it is necessary to know, the following questions:

---

[1] A set of technical and administrative knowledge that is essential to carry out a commercial process and that is not protected by a patent.

How do you access the tacit knowledge that employees have?

How do you motivate, encourage commitment and identification with the organization's values?

How do you get the experts, the professionals (who are often found to be the most resistant to change) to get involved and accept the changes?

How do you manage the experts' time, since managing knowledge always involves a dedication that is sometimes difficult to manage?

How do you change the culture based on 'knowledge is power'? [22]

"Thus, Nonaka and Takeuchi (1995) propose that the creation of new knowledge depends on the vision, perception, personal intuition and that, for this, the commitment of the people who work in the organization is key. They also talk about the vital role that teams have in the creation of knowledge and the role of management, which has the task of promoting the acquisition, production, use and transfer of knowledge. "" [22]

"Knowledge management appears as a weapon to minimize the loss of intellectual capital that can occur when people leave. In relation to this, it is proposed to create a culture within the organization, so that each member stores what he or she has learned in each work process, and is able to transmit it. That is, to make knowledge capture a step in the key processes of knowledge management (Bosch 2002). "" [22]

"As for what is understood by knowledge management, Esteban and Navarro (2003) propose that knowledge management is, therefore, the discipline that deals with research, development, application and innovation of procedures and instruments necessary for the creation of knowledge in organizations, in order to increase their value and competitive advantage. The object of its practice is the construction of a knowledge production system useful in an organization for decision making and the resolution of its strategic business processes, linked to its objectives and corporate values and its strategic plan through the design, implementation, maintenance and evaluation of a program for the identification, conservation, organization, integration, analysis, assessment, protection, sharing and effective use of the information resources available to it and the intellectual capital of its members, with the support of information and communication technologies (ICT). "" [22]

"As can be seen, it is a definition that covers everything from the creation of knowledge to its transfer for the good of the company, and is thus associated with business intelligence processes, and the need for ICT support. "" [22]

"Ortiz de Urbina (2003) offers a definition that relates knowledge management to intellectual capital, understood as the intangible resources of the organization. Knowledge management is understood as the set of processes that use knowledge to identify and exploit the intangible resources in the company, as well as to generate new ones. It is given by the union of the activities and specific initiatives that are carried out to increase its volume of corporate knowledge. "" [22]

"This same author states that in this way, knowledge management constitutes a flow variable through which a certain amount of intellectual capital is transformed into another. The result is a new dimension of intellectual capital. Figure 1 tries to represent these relationships by showing how intellectual capital is both the input and output of knowledge management, since this part of a certain level of knowledge that, through better use, manages to reach a new and higher level of knowledge. "" [22]

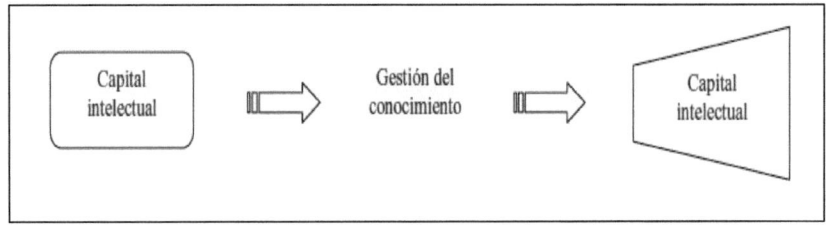

Figure 1

Intellectual capital and knowledge management (Ortiz de Urbina 2003) Source. Extracted from [22]

According to Fernandez (2000), "organizations that develop knowledge management have the following common features:

-       Ability to unite, to generate a strong sense of identity.

-       Sensitivity to the environment in order to learn and adapt

-       Tolerance of unconventional thinking and experience.

-       Financial precaution, to retain the resources that ensure the essential flexibility in the current environment. "

"Regarding the objectives that can be achieved with knowledge management, Pavez (2000), cites the following:

-       Formulate an organizational outreach strategy for the development, acquisition and application of knowledge

-       Implementing knowledge-oriented strategies.

-       Promote the continuous improvement of business processes with emphasis on the generation and use of knowledge.

-       Follow and evaluate the achievements obtained with the application of knowledge.

-       Reduce cycle times in the development of new products, improvements to existing ones, and in the development of solutions to problems.

-       Reduce costs associated with repeated errors.

From the above, it is clear that knowledge management is the basis for carrying out the other organizational processes -say intellectual capital management and acquisition of organizational learning-, once this is a concrete part of the organization, the other processes will be aware by all members and obviously the institution will be able to learn more, through a process of continuous improvement. The benefits obtained from knowledge management lead to the improvement of the services and products of the institution, to the extent that these are the result of the existing knowledge both in the environment and in the internal organizational level. "

"Within an organization or company, intellectual capital is the intellectual knowledge of that organization, the intangible information (which is not visible, and therefore is not collected anywhere) that it possesses and can produce value. " [Wikipedia]

"Table 2 explains the differences between tacit and explicit knowledge. It is important to note that new knowledge is generated in the dynamic interaction and combination of these two types (Nonaka and Takeuchi, 1995). "" [7]

Table 2

Subject: Differences between tacit and explicit knowledge

	Tácito (subjetivo)	Explícito (objetivo)
Conocimiento	Se orienta a la acción y es personal, lo que hace difícil su formalización y comunicación.	Este puede ser formulado, resumido y transmitido en el espacio independientemente del conocimiento de las disciplinas.
Trasmisión del conocimiento	Requiere interacción estrecha entre los individuos y a través de elsta llegan a un entendimiento común y confianza entre ellos.	Verbal o escrita.
Adquisición y acumulación del conocimiento	Solamente a través de la experiencia práctica (aprender haciendo).	Se puede generar mediante deducción lógica y se adquiere por medio del estudio formal.

Fuente: Elaboración propia a partir de Nonaka y Takeuchi (1995).

Source. Extracted from [7]

Fundamentals of the pedagogical knowledge management model at the university

"Knowledge management has traditionally been applied as a theory or tool to business organizations, giving rise to recognized models such as Nonaka and Takeuchi in 1995, Anderson in 1998, among many others. Educational institutions and universities as part of these, in recent years have launched initiatives for knowledge management that is generated from the processes that take place within them. "'' [20]

"Knowledge management establishes four stages in its generation cycle: capture, contextualization, socialization and application/generation. Through the development of this cycle, which occurs in each of the sources mentioned above, pedagogical knowledge is constantly converted from tacit to explicit and vice versa, this process leads to a process of individual and organizational learning. "'' [20]

Introduction

"Pedagogical knowledge is a complex resource and of a tacit nature that is expressed in the organized set of data, information, experience and know-how that is generated in the pedagogical field. It is a strategically relevant resource in Higher Education, since it directly impacts on the training processes through the transformations and decision-making in the formation of professionals and the pedagogical improvement of teachers. Unlike what happens with information, pedagogical knowledge is intrinsic to the teacher, and its capture, socialization, contextualization and generation occur as part of the interaction between the different subjects involved in the process. Moreover, it generates synergies and is not disregarded over time, but rather is consolidated, thus constituting the organizational pedagogical memory. "" [17]

Development

"The process of formation of university professionals requires from the teachers a preparation that goes beyond the knowledge of the subject they teach, that is to say, the handling of pedagogical elements that allow the development of competences in the students and the continuous improvement of the Higher Education, the previous is materialized in the process of management of pedagogical knowledge in the university. "" [20]

Knowledge management in education

"In recent years, knowledge management has gained strength in the area of education, educational institutions have begun to articulate it in the process of teaching and learning. The philosophy of teaching and learning is not about how knowledge is transferred from teachers to students, but how students can design and create new knowledge from the knowledge that has been shaped through books, articles, magazines, electronic media, etc. "" [20]

"Knowledge management [38] in education seeks the integration of all human resources, academic processes and technological advances, involved in the design, capture and execution of the intellectual infrastructure of an educational institution. The approach is based on the elaboration and academic management to learn while maintaining the balance between the various entities in an academic environment. "" [20]

Knowledge management models in education

"Different authors have addressed the issue of knowledge management models in education. Of them we can highlight the approach. This author proposes a model of knowledge management in education that is composed of eight modules that interact and feed back from the central module. This central module called knowledge management uses human competencies, experiences, knowledge, skills, talents, thoughts, ideas, commitments, innovations, practices and integrates them with the information and resources that the organization uses to achieve its strategic objectives. The other modules allow knowledge acquisition, evaluation, use of knowledge, knowledge dissemination, storage, learning, leadership using information technologies, strengthening the learning processes in the educational organization, instilling in people the ability to create and provide the organizational climate, so that the acquisition of knowledge is efficient. However, this model does not clearly define the characteristics of the ICT used, which does not allow identifying the use of e-learning tools in the implementation. Additionally, it is not clear in the model if it is directed to higher education, face-to-face and autonomous modality. "" [20]

"The demand for educational models [10] in the post-modern era is the new ways of teaching and learning, in mixed learning contexts [classroom + virtual]. The development of educational platforms, as part of such contexts, requires the consideration of epistemological and technological design models, which allow for effective pedagogical work environments. Virtual learning scenarios can be formed as intelligent communities, capable of thinking about themselves and managing their knowledge, complementing classroom teaching with virtual teaching. It is necessary to associate the curricular integration of information and communication technologies with notions of knowledge management, to add epistemological value to the use of technologies for learning. Also, to consider and solve the complexity of the design of these environments, it is necessary to apply a development methodology that is incremental, interdisciplinary and scalable, ensuring that the communicational, pedagogical, didactic, technological and management aspects have been duly considered and solved in a balanced way. "" [20]

2.3.4. Knowledge Management Models

a.   Knowledge Creation Process (Nonaka, Takeuchi, 1995)
"We can explain the concept of knowledge as the process of absorbing, adopting and internalizing information in each of us: it is about learning and apprehending information. "" [23]

"From this perspective, knowledge has two visible qualities: it is something that can be **stored, either in** a physical or psychic way - by internalizing it - and it is something that **flows, in the** sense that it can be communicated and transmitted between people through different means or media, for example, through dialogue and writing. Perhaps it is precisely this double aspect of something static/dynamic that makes its treatment and management complicated.
-     **Tacit** knowledge is that which is not physically palpable, but is internal and the property of each person in particular.

-     **Explicit** knowledge is that which can be expressed or represented by physically storable and transmissible symbols. "" [23]

"The dynamic and constant mechanism of relationship between tacit knowledge and explicit knowledge is constituted as the basis of the model (see figure 2):

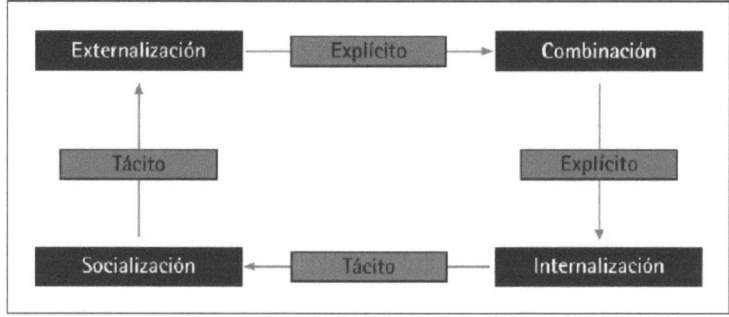

Figure 2

Title: Processes of Knowledge Conversion in the Organization (Nonaka and Takeuchi, 1995) Source. Extracted from [23]

-       **Socialization** is the process by which individuals learn to function in their social environment, acquiring tacit knowledge through the common channels of relationship and communication with people and media such as conversations, documentation consultation, etc. is one of the most important aspects that companies care about today: communication management oriented to the transmission of information with the aim of acquiring knowledge about something that the organization itself does not have but through its members or employees. ""' [23]

-       "**Externalization** is the process of knowing how to transmit and conceptualize the tacit knowledge that people possess internally. It uses elements that are tangible and understandable to several people: those who want to teach and those who want to learn. It is one of the most important issues and perhaps the basic one for the survival of companies: the transmission of knowledge between an employee who knows and another who does not know and wants to learn. An optimal way for this flow of knowledge to be achieved is through group work. Through it, from the synergy of existing tacit knowledge in the group will be born a knowledge physically formalizable. ""' [23]

- "**Combination** is the explicit formalization of knowledge from various sources of information. The fruit must be also explicit and storable information. It is a question of obtaining a recasting of new explicit knowledge obtained from other explicit knowledge already existing. "" [23]

- "Finally, **interiorization** is a process of acquiring explicit knowledge that can reach us from different supports or means, so that it becomes something that is ours, our own and internal to each and every one of us. The person is then aware of what he or she has to learn and directs his or her effort to apprehend it. "" [23]

"Knowledge, then, is created in an organization through a continuous process of conversion of the two basic types of knowledge in the successive phases of socialization, externalization, combination and internalization. Each time you go around the four quadrants of the previous graph, new knowledge is generated. In each quadrant, the conversion problems are different and can be more or less complex depending on the company or organization being addressed. Any company interested in the management and creation of knowledge must somehow promote a climate that favors the dynamism represented in the graph. "" [23]

b.   *"Arthur Andersen Model (Arthur Andersen, 1999)" [23]*

"This model is based on the idea of **favoring the transmission of information that is valuable to the** organization. This movement of information will go from the **individuals to the organization, and from there it will travel back to the individuals** again. The underlying objective is to create value that customers can see and recognize, so that customers will bet more on the company in question. "" [23]

"The novelties of the model refer to two aspects:"

"On the one hand, at the individual level, because there is a personal responsibility to share and make explicit the knowledge that one possesses, an ethical obligation towards the rest of the colleagues in the organization; and on the other hand, at the organizational level, because the management of the company must bet and lead a climate that promotes that individual level mentioned". 23] (See Figure 3).

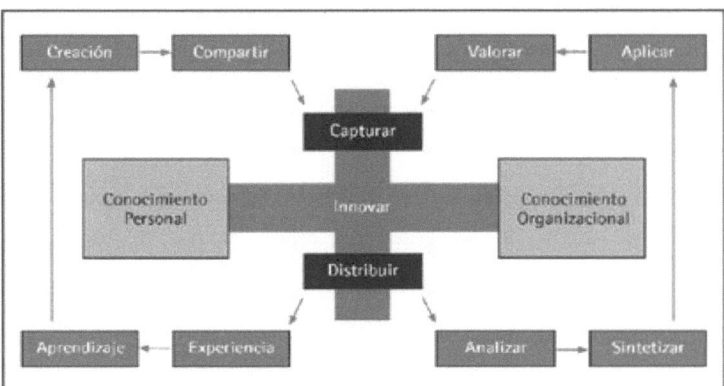

Figure 3

Title: "Knowledge Management Model Arthur Andersen (1999).
Source. "Arthur Andersen (1999). "
Source. Extracted from [23]

"To favor this flow of information, two mechanisms are established: **networks to share knowledge,** which are physical or virtual places where professionals can share their experiences, allowing communication, learning, and ultimately the transfer of knowledge between people; and **knowledge packaged** or encapsulated, through an internal system called Arthur Andersen Knowledge Space, which has various documentation (methodologies, experiences, examples,...) and is available to the members of the company. "" [23]

c.   *"Knowledge Management Assessment Tool (KMAT)" [23]*

"The KMAT, Knowledge Management Assessment Tool, is based on the **Organizational Knowledge Management** Model jointly created by Arthur Andersen and APQC" [23] (see figure 4):

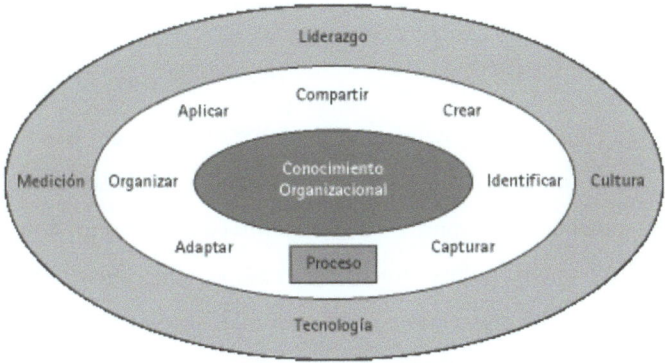

Figure 4

Knowledge Management Assessment Tool (KMAT) model. Source Arthur Andersen (1999). Source: Arthur Andersen (1999). Taken from [23].

Related to this model are a series of concepts: **leadership,** which refers to the way in which the company leads its business or field of action; **culture,** as a climate that the organization has for the areas of teaching and new learning; **technology, which** takes note of the means of communication that the company provides to its employees; **measurement, which** measures the intellectual capital and the relationship of resources oriented to its growth; and **processes**, which is related to the internal mechanics of location, transmission and acquisition of knowledge. ""' [23]

d.   *"Knowledge Cluster Model (Basque Country)" [23]*

"This meeting point for knowledge and experiences is formed by Universities, Business Schools, a multitude of Companies and other organizations. Its raison d'être is based on improving business competitiveness, and is made up of different clusters: Business Management, Environmental Industries, Telecommunications..." [23]

"We see that the Cluster of Knowledge in Business Management was born to detect and give notoriety and application to that knowledge in business management that is the most suitable for improving competitiveness among companies and organizations. As main points since its creation, the cluster will facilitate communication between the various elements of it, support an improvement in quality, offer training and emphasize the importance that companies have to give the desire to acquire knowledge. "" [23]

"To achieve this, two lines of action have been detailed: one through the actions of dynamization, which are those that are defined as priorities by the Strategic Plan created from the executive management of the Cluster; and the other achieved from the stakeholders, which are focuses or meeting points for the members of the Knowledge Cluster. They have several knowledge areas, such as Research and Modeling of Knowledge Management and Improvement of Knowledge Dissemination in Management. "" [23]

e.   *KPMG Consulting's Knowledge Management Model (Tejedor and Aguirre, 1998)*

"Starting from what are the conditioning factors involved in learning, as well as the result itself and the fruit of any learning that occurs, this company creates a model that explains two of the most important factors when talking about knowledge management:

the **conditioning factors of learning,** and the **expected learning outcomes**. ""
[23]

"The following chart illustrates precisely the basic concepts set forth by this model:

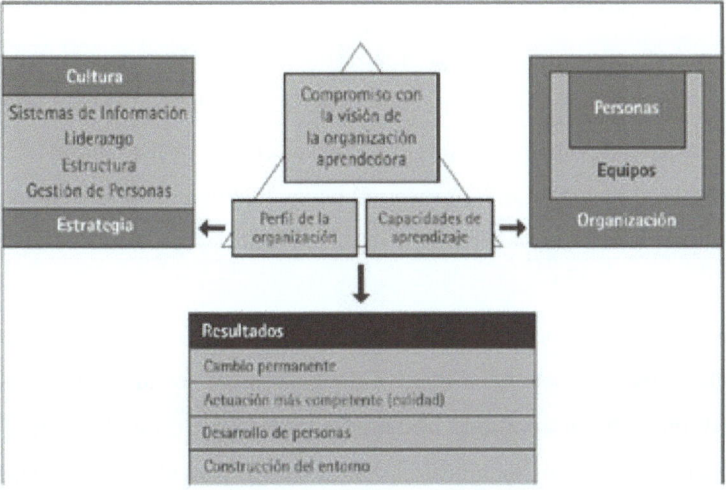

Figure 5

KPMG's Knowledge Management Model Source: Weaver and Aguirre (1998). Source: Tejedor and Aguirre (1998). Extracted from [23].

The factors that actively intervene in learning in an organization are: the existence of a clear **commitment** clearly led by the management of the company, which will have assimilated the need for knowledge management to meet the objectives of the company; the existence of **climates that encourage learning,** since the members of the organization must be located in an environment that favors training and exchange of experiences; and the existence of **infrastructures that** allow the company to function optimally in all its aspects: management, production, human resources,...". [23]

"As a result of this acquired knowledge, we can make a list of results that should be easily palpable: the evolution and flexibility of the company, the improvement in quality, as well as the personal and professional development of its employees would be some of these aspects. "" [23]

2.3.5. Nonaka and Takeuchi's SECI Knowledge Creation Model

"SECI" stands for Socialization, Externalization, Combination and Interiorization. Each one of these four words represents processes, of which only some of them and in a very superficial way are present in the development of the laboratory courses. What is proposed is that all these processes be applied in a conscious and sustained manner. "" [14]

"Lopez G. (et. al [2]) defines: Socialization (tacit to tacit): knowledge is transferred fundamentally by experience, so that, in the process of socialization, experiences are shared through observation, imitation, practice or through discussions, to produce mental models or technical skills. Because it involves the acceptance of beliefs, feelings, and emotions of others, it is very difficult to achieve without personal, face-to-face contact, and for this very reason requires individuals to empathize with each other (Rynes et al., 2001). "" [14]

"Externalization" (tacitly stated): is associated with the creation of concepts. "The tacit mental model is verbalized in words and phrases, and finally crystallized in explicit concepts..." (Nonaka and Takeuchi, 1995). In this phase the teams reflect collectively, using different methods of reasoning: induction, deduction and abduction, but, above all, the latter employs the figurative language of metaphors and analogiesii. The authors attribute the key to the creation of new knowledge to

---

[2] "And others"

externalization, since it is the process in which concepts are formed explicitly and because of the methods it requires. "" [14]

" Combination (Explicit to Explicit): it is a process of systematization of information and concepts, in which the existing information is reconfigured and which starts with one or several justified concepts. These are expressed in the organizational intention, in the vision or in the strategy (Explicit Knowledge), to arrive at a prototype of product or service (Explicit Knowledge), with the competence of different experts of the organization (Research and Development, market, quality control, etc.), or also to arrive at a new model of an organizational process or a new structure (Explicit Knowledge) where teams from all organizational areas intervene. "" [14]

" Internalization (Explicit to tacit): the existence of explicit knowledge does not guarantee its assimilation and incorporation into the mental structure and it is here where the process of internalization takes relevance, because until knowledge has been incorporated individually, it is not possible to continue the process of knowledge creation, because, although group processes exist, it is people themselves who produce the new knowledge. "" [14]

2.3.6. Knowledge Management Tools as Solution Options to the Problem of Knowledge Harnessing in the Computer Lab

"The literature specialized in information sciences and other related sciences shows the conformation of a theoretical-conceptual field referred to the tools of knowledge mapping. These include two trends: authors who use and name the tool for knowledge management, concept mapping (Ausubel *et al.* 1989 and Rovira 2006), and others who call it knowledge mapping, including it in the specific processes of knowledge auditing (KA). Both are framed in the organizational level (D' Alós-Moner'2003, Núñez 2006, Anon 2008 and Piloto 2008). "" [22]

"Today's society - called the Information Society (Castell 2001), the Information and Knowledge Society (Bell 1973) or the Society of Organizations (Drucker 1995) - is influenced by the processes and approaches of knowledge management because, according to Boisot (1998), it resembles a practice more than an intellectual discipline in itself. Thus, we see a new society that combines, on the one hand, management, conceived as human action, voluntary and determined in resources to achieve a particular goal. On the other hand, the knowledge, like intellectual human act that allows to know the nature, characteristics and qualities of an action or thing (López 2006). ''" [22]

"Since the late 1980s, Ausubel *et al.* (1989) have been creating concept maps, with the aim of understanding the level of learning and association of a group of students. Until today it has been demonstrated the importance of these in knowledge management practices and its more concrete evolution in knowledge maps, specifically linked to the knowledge audit approach (Pilot 2008). ''" [22]

"Both are knowledge management tools that have been applied in learning organizations and positive results have been obtained (Rovira and Mesa 2006). In this way, concept maps are the precursors of what is known today as knowledge mapping, where the principles and theory of both terms are interwoven to enrich knowledge management. ''" [22]

2.4. Hypothesis Formulation

2.4.1. General Hypothesis

The absence of knowledge management methods and tools for software production in a computer laboratory of the Faculty of Systems and Computer Engineering of San Marcos University influences its low specialized production and quality.

2.4.2. Specific Hypotheses

- The absence of a knowledge management method in a computer lab makes it difficult to identify essential information on which to base software solutions for students in a specific and massive way.

- The lack of a history of results and a documentary database makes it difficult for students to record, save and reuse software and to maintain order and discipline in software development in a specific and massive way.

- The lack of support and advice from specialists and experts in software development makes it difficult for students to devote themselves to developing software on a massive scale.

2.4.3. Identification of Variables

2.4.3.1. Independent Variable

Knowledge management methods and tools.

2.4.3.2. Dependent Variable

Software production.

Table 3

Title: Operationalization of research variables

Variable	Dimension	Indicator	Unit of measurement
Independent: Knowledge management methods and tools	History of results	Text documents	Quantity
		Software modules	Quantity
	Documentary database	Text documents	Quantity
		Unstructured project data	No. of projects
			No. of modules
	Expert Directory	List of expert knowledge holders	Number of experts
			No. of areas of knowledge
			No. of problems solved
Dependent: Software production		Level of knowledge	Yes
			No

Source. Own elaboration

Table 4

Subject: Consistency matrix

General problem	General objective	General hypothesis	Variables	Data collection technique
What is the effect of producing software without applying a knowledge management method or tool in a computer laboratory of the San Marcos University School of Systems and Computer Engineering?	Determine which knowledge management methods and tools are applied for the production of software in a computer laboratory of the Faculty of Systems and Computer Engineering of San Marcos University.	The absence of knowledge management methods and tools in a computer laboratory of the San Marcos University's School of Systems and Computer Engineering influences the low production of software.	**Independent variable**: knowledge management methods and tools.	A questionnaire and indirect observation were used and the results were recorded in a simple list during the activities. The recording was in a simple list due to difficulties of observation to be able to do it in a total and complete way.
Specific problems	**Specific Objectives**	**Specific hypotheses**		
1. What is the consequence of producing software without a knowledge	1. Determine which knowledge management method teachers apply to produce software in a computer lab at	1. The absence of a knowledge management method in a computer lab makes it	**Dependent variable**: software production.	

81

management tool that allows the documentation of the created software to facilitate its reuse? 2. What is the consequence of producing software in a computer lab without leaving a record of the functionality and usefulness of the software created and that it can be reused? 3. What is the consequence of producing software without the assistance, advice and support of people with	the Faculty. 2. Determine which knowledge management tool is applied in a computer lab that allows to leave a record and evidence of the existence, functionality and usefulness of the software created. 3. Determine which knowledge management tool is used in a computer lab that allows communication with experts in programming and with the experience and capacity necessary to guide in the creation of software.	difficult to identify essential information on which to base software solutions for students in a specific and massive way. 2. The lack of a history of results and a documentary database makes it difficult for students to record, save and reuse software and to maintain order and discipline in software development in a specific and massive way. 3. The lack of		

more experience and knowledge in software development and in the need, applicability and usefulness of it?		support and advice from specialists and experts in software development makes it difficult for students to devote themselves to developing software on a massive scale.		

Source. Own elaboration

Chapter 3. Methodology

3.1. Description of the Research

Below are the elements of the methodology used in the research. The elements such as the structure were taken from the internet address: https://www.youtube.com/watch?v=6RwYCEZgoM4 which I consider clearly and orderly defines the steps followed.

This study was conducted with students who took lab courses from the lowest to the highest cycle where at least one software production lab course was scheduled. The aim was to know the existence of knowledge management methods and tools for software production in a computer laboratory of the Faculty of Systems Engineering and Computer Science of San Marcos University.

3.2. Research Design

Since the independent variable observed is not manipulated and there is no control over it, it is a non-experimental, transversal-exploratory research.

3.3. Research Approach

This study is considered a quantitative approach. 48] It states: "The important thing is not to know the entire list of possible designs, but to appeal to logical reasoning and experience to determine, before collecting the data, what information a particular method will provide and what relevance and reliability can be assigned to it. "

3.4. Population

The study was aimed at the student population of the Faculty of Systems Engineering and Computer Science at San Marcos University.

3.5. Sample Size

Taking into account that the laboratory courses are given in three shifts and the access to each one of those laboratories is almost impossible, it was decided to carry out a survey at the moment they were in the classroom and with the respective authorization of the professor, we proceeded to carry it out, managing to survey a total of 314 students of the 2018-II semester; this work was complemented with a period of observation in the way they developed their lab work and the way they interacted with the technological resources.

In our case the sample is considered to be a non-probability sample due to some circumstances that prevent access to the whole population and the way each activity or class session is developed in a laboratory.

3.6. Type of Sampling

The type of sampling used was simple random sampling.

3.7. Research Techniques

The questionnaire and observation were used.

3.8. Data Collection Instruments

According to the technique used, a questionnaire with closed questions was used and the objective was to obtain answers from the units of analysis regarding methods and tools of knowledge management used during the laboratory classes to produce software. Some of the variables studied were

- Implicit knowledge.
- Explicit knowledge.
- Knowledge management tools.
- Computer resources.

3.9. Data Analysis Techniques

Once the data collection was completed, the following actions were taken:

- Coding and data logging.
- Use of SPSS and Excel software.
- Presentation of the results in tables and figures.

Chapter 4. Results and discussion

4.1. Analysis, Interpretation and Discussion of Results

Among the academic articles cited there is some agreement in what is manifested in "ICT Tools and Knowledge Management" [1], in "University Students, ICTs and Learning" [2], in "Considerations on the Use of Information Technologies in University Education" [6], in "Progressive Innovation and Virtualization of Latin American Universities Towards the Knowledge Society" [16], in "Model for the Development of Knowledge Management in Public University Research Centers. Caso Aplicativo Universidad Pedagógica y Tecnológica de Colombia (UPTC)" [18].

These articles express in general that if there are no knowledge management methods or tools to guide the management and administration of information and knowledge, little or nothing can be achieved to optimize and increase the software production of a university whose essential existence is precisely the generation of knowledge.

The difference between the academic articles cited with this research is that none of them specifically refers to the fact that the explicit application of knowledge management methods and tools will allow the mass production of software, as proposed in this study, but let's not forget that the software produced in a university is also part of its intellectual production.

4.1.1. Descriptive analysis of the data

The following figures show the results of the descriptive statistics of the survey carried out to a sample of 314 students from an approximate of more than 1400 students from different courses, shifts, cycles and sexes in the School of Systems Engineering and Computer Science of San Marcos University of the 2018-II cycle;

in addition, some others are mentioned among the main indicators, only as a reference to complement and make the analysis more understandable. An interpretation of the result of each indicator is also tested:

Indicator 1: distribution of students per shift in which he took a laboratory course.

Figure 6

Character: distribution of students with laboratory courses in shifts. Source. Own elaboration

Interpretation:
The late shift concentrates the largest number of students with a laboratory course.

Indicator 2: academic cycle in which the greatest number of students who took a laboratory course are concentrated.

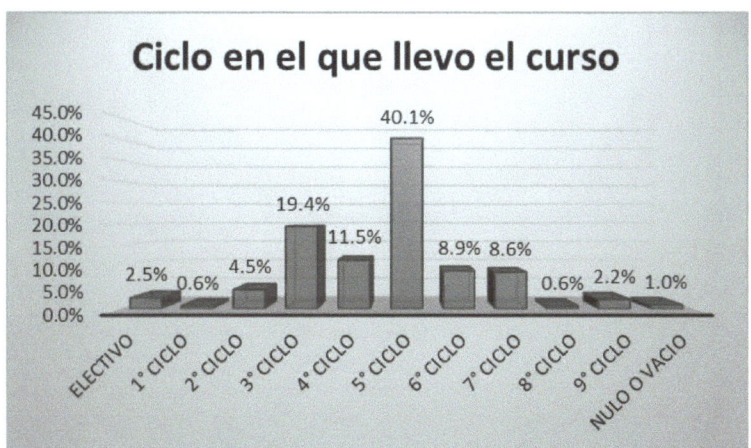

Figure 7

Character: distribution of students with laboratory courses per cycle. Source. Own elaboration

Interpretation:

The fifth cycle concentrates the largest number of students who took a laboratory course.

Indicator 3: students who claim to have recognized and used some knowledge management tools in their sessions in a laboratory.

Figure 8

Title: % of students familiar with knowledge management tools.

Source. Own elaboration

Interpretation:

4.8% of students recognized that they are familiar with some knowledge management tool.

Indicator 4: Students who report using a history of laboratory results

Figure 9

Title: % of students who have used a history of results. Source. Own elaboration

Interpretation:

18.5% of students say they have used a history of results in a computer lab.

Indicator 5: Students who report using a documentary Database in a laboratory.

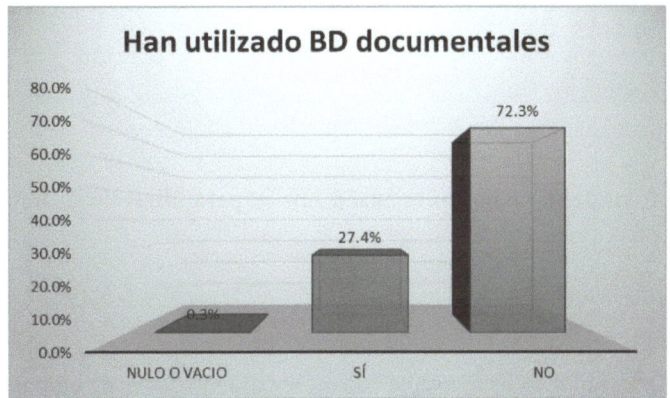

Figure 10

Title: % of students who have used BD documentaries. Source. Own elaboration

Interpretation:

27.4% of students say they have used a documentary database in a computer lab.

Indicator 6: Students who report having access to a directory of experts in their lab sessions.

Figure 11

Title: % of students who have used an expert directory. Source. Own elaboration

Interpretation:

3.5% of students say they have used a "directory of experts" in a computer lab.

Indicator 7: Students who say that new knowledge resulting from their own research, work or deduction has been stored in a DB managed by the faculty and has served new generations of students and teachers.

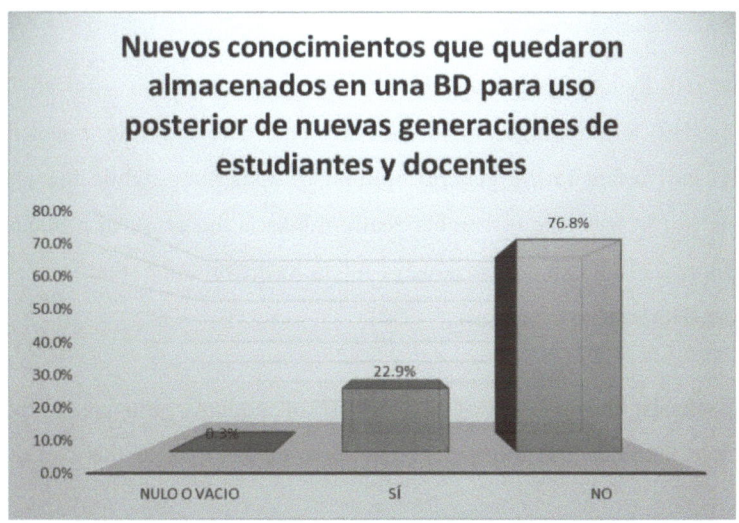

Figure 12

Character: % of pupils whose new knowledge is stored. Source. Own elaboration

Interpretation:

22.9% of students said that their new knowledge acquired through their own research was recorded and stored in a database for later use by any user.

4.1.2. Inferential analysis of the data

4.1.2.1. Hypothesis testing

Having as an assumption that the main previous indicators have not been used in the software creation process, the hypothesis test is analyzed to demonstrate that there is a deficiency in the application of knowledge management methods and tools in the academic activities in a computer laboratory and it is necessary to reconsider them in order to increase software production.

4.1.2.2. Hypothesis approach

"Next, the null hypothesis H0 and the alternative hypothesis Ha are raised. The null hypothesis (H0) is a hypothesis that the researcher tries to refute, reject or annul. Generally, null refers to the general opinion of something, while the alternative hypothesis (Ha) is what the researcher really thinks is the cause of a phenomenon. The conclusion of an experiment always refers to the null one, that is, it rejects or accepts the (H0) instead of the (Ha). "" [50]

Null hypothesis: the average of the sample of students who apply knowledge management methods and tools to obtain software is equal to the average of the population.

$$H_0: \square = \mu$$

Alternative hypothesis: The average of the sample of students who apply knowledge management methods and tools to create software is different from the average of the population.

$$Ha: \square \neq \mu$$

Choose the level of significance (α):

" This is defined as the "maximum amount of error we are willing to accept in order to give the researcher's hypothesis as valid. "50] See the following table.

Table 5

Title: Levels of significance and confidence

Significance Level (α)	Confidence level
0.05	0.95

Source. Own elaboration

" It is considered a 95% reliability, with a significance level of 0.05 which is the most used significance level. "50] (see table 6)

Table 6

Title: parameters for the calculation of the Z of the sample

μ	1
Average ( )	0.10
Standard deviation (σ)	0.430
Sample (n)	314
Significance Level (α)	0.05

Source. Own elaboration

Calculation of the Z of the sample:

$$Z = \frac{\bar{X} - \mu}{\frac{S}{\sqrt{n}}}$$

$$Z = 0.10 - 1/ (0.43/\sqrt{314})$$

$$Z = -37.09$$

It is observed that Z falls into the "hypothesis rejection zone", therefore, the null hypothesis is rejected and the alternative hypothesis is accepted. The result is shown graphically below, as well as its interpretation (see figure 13):

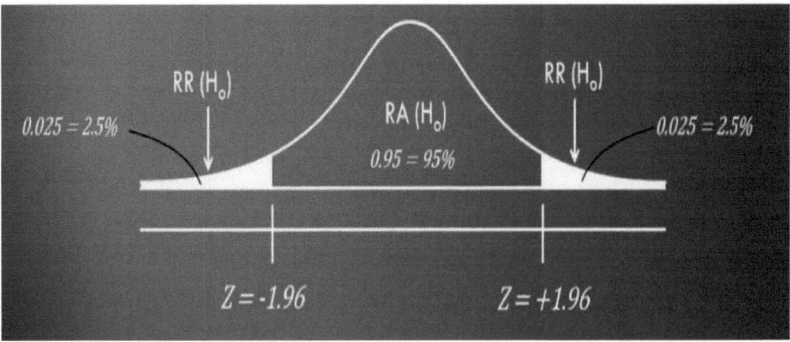

Figure 13

Title: Normal distribution curve for hypothesis testing. Source. Extracted from the web address:

https://www.youtube.com/watch?v=AJcy4eZMwWM)

Interpretation:

"To the right of the critical negative Z is located the "acceptance zone" which means that if the Z value of the sample falls into that zone then the null hypothesis is accepted (H0) and the alternative hypothesis is rejected (Ha). If the Z value of the sample falls into the "rejection zone", then the null hypothesis is rejected (H0) and the alternative hypothesis is accepted (Ha). "" [50]. In words, this means for H0: "the average number of students who use knowledge management methods and tools to create software in a computer laboratory is different from the average number of the population", therefore, the implementation of knowledge management methods and tools in a computer laboratory would optimize the process of software creation and, therefore, of software.

4.2. Presentation of Results

The present study conducted a survey research in the Faculty to know which methods and tools of knowledge management are explicitly applied in a computer laboratory that contributes to increase the production of knowledge and particularly software. Variables were analyzed that gave us an indication of the use, application and exploitation of knowledge management methods and tools; attention was paid to some knowledge management method and some tools.

In the results of all the variables analyzed there is a quite significant difference between those who perceive and recognize the methods and tools and for whom the use of such methods and tools goes unnoticed. A large percentage of students use these methods and tools unconsciously, unaware that they can be better utilized for software production by using any of the methods suggested in this document, such as Nonaka's and Takeuchi's SECI method, which would help improve knowledge production, particularly software.

Conclusions

This research concludes on the basis of the results obtained that the methods and tools of knowledge management applied in a computer laboratory of the Faculty of Systems and Computer Engineering to produce software are invisible or implicit in the didactic strategy and this affirmation is based on the percentages obtained in the results of the survey, whose questionnaire elaborated with closed questions, allowed evaluating the following indicators:

- "Students familiar with knowledge management methods".
- What tools do you apply in a computer lab to record and record the existence, functionality and usefulness of the software?
- What knowledge management tool do you apply to have the advice of experts in programming and with the experience and capacity necessary to guide in the creation of software?

This transectional-exploratory study was the first effort to obtain an initial idea of the importance of making knowledge management methods and tools visible in order to better guide students in the production of software in the Faculty. This study does not constitute an exhaustive analysis, it only implies a first approach that in the future should be deepened in the studied environment and of course improved and extended.

Recommendations

Similar studies are recommended to reinforce the idea of implementing QA methods and tools involving software production with the intention of further improving its quality. This research, based on the results obtained, recommends making visible the explicit application of knowledge management methods and tools to produce software and evaluating which methods and tools would be best adapted to make them visible and used explicitly in computer laboratories with the aim of producing software in a more intensive and specialized way, seeking a competitive advantage over other universities. The teachers responsible for establishing a teaching strategy, together with ICT tools, should focus on an ambitious purpose such as leading the Faculty to be a reference in this activity.

Research that would be important to consider:

• First, to consider the possibility of implementing the use of technological tools in the classrooms in general, but based on a renewed intentionality of the teaching-learning process.

• Second, to investigate how to reinforce the preparation of teachers in the application of technological tools in their classrooms due precisely to the novelty and the dizzying way in which technology evolves.

• Third, to promote the management and production of software in the laboratories with the aim of producing it based on international standards or ISO norms.

Bibliographic references

1] Quintanilla Juárez, N. (2014). ICT tools and knowledge management. *Universidad Don Bosco, calle al plan del pino, Soyapango. El Salvador*, accessed February 20, 2017 on the World Wide Web: http://rd.udb.edu.sv:8080/jspui/bitstream/11715/621/1/Herramientas%20TICs%20y%20Gestion.pdf

2] Zalazar, D. F., & Neri, C. (2013). University students, ICTs and learning. Research Yearbook, 20, 153-158.

3] Faustino, A., Pérez S. (2013). Interdisciplinarity of science and applied social research No. 11 - December 2013 -pp. 0-31 || Thematic Section Received: 25/1/2013 - Accepted: 28/11/2013

[4] Rivero, C., Chávez, A., Vásquez, A., & Blumen, S. (2016). ICTs in university education. Achievements and challenges for training in psychology and education. *Revista de Psicología, 34*(1), 185-199. doi:http://dx.doi.org/10.18800/psico.201601.007

5] Lic. Guillermo Enrique Farell Vázquez. National Center for Technical and Health Professional Improvement (CENAPET). Double street S. Francisco and carriageway Aldabó. Arroyo Naranjo. Havana City. Received: January 18th, 2002. Approved: February 17th, 2002.

6] Chaparro quoting: Angel Arbonies. "Knowledge to innovate". Madrid, MIK, 2006. p26.

[7]   Zambrano Vargas, S., & Quitián Rodríguez, L. (2015). Analysis of knowledge management in a higher education institution. Criterio Libre, 13(22), 279-297. https://doi.org/10.18041/1900-0642/criteriolibre.2015v13n22.140

[8]   http://epistemologia2008.blogspot.com/2008/04/epistemologa-de-la-educacin.html

12] Estrada Sentí, V., & Benítez Cárdenas, F. (2013). Knowledge management in the new Cuban university. *University Pedagogy, 11*(2). Retrieved from http://cvi.mes.edu.cu/peduniv/index.php/peduniv/article/view/361

13] R. Balmori, C. Schemelkes. "*Knowledge Management in Higher Education*". Sinectica, Electronic Journal of Education. Jan 2012, Issue 38, p1.

14] López G., M., & Cabrales G., F., & Schmal S., R. (2005). Knowledge Management: A Theoretical Review and its Association with the University. *Panorama Socioeconómico, (30), 0.*

[15]   M. Mejía, M. Colin. "*Knowledge Management and its importance in the organizations*". Trilogy Magazine N° 9. Jul 2013, p1.

[16]   Casas Armengol, M., & Stojanovic, L. (2005). Progressive innovation and virtualization of Latin American universities towards the knowledge society. *RIED. Revista Iberoamericana de Educación a Distancia, 8*(1-2), 127-146. doi:https://doi.org/10.5944/ried.1.8.1060

17] Páez Paredes, I., & Díaz Domínguez, D. (2013). Fundamentals of the pedagogical knowledge management model for the University of Pinar del Rio. Foundations of knowledge management model for teaching the University of Pinar del Rio... *University Congress,* Consulted by http://www.congresouniversidad.cu/revista/index.php/rcu/article/view/397

[18]   J. González, "*Modelo para el Desarrollo de la Gestión del Conocimiento en los Centros de Investigación de la Universidades Públicas Colombianas. Case Study of the Universidad Pedagógica y Tecnológica de Colombia (UPTC)*". Management and Strategy No. 35, January / June 2009

[19]   Torres, K., & Lamenta, P. (2015). KNOWLEDGE MANAGEMENT AND INFORMATION SYSTEMS IN ORGANIZATIONS. *Negotium, 11* (32), 3-20.

[20]   R. Escobar, Dr. C. Montenegro, W. Joven, Mag. "*Knowledge management models that integrate e-learning technologies in higher education*". ISSN: 2248 - 762X | Vol. 4 | Special Edition | Pages 103-113 | September 2013

[21]   Saz, Miguel Angel del. "Knowledge management: pros and cons". In: El profesional de la información, 2001, April, v. 10, n. 4, pp. 14-28.

[22]   Caraballo, Y., & Mesa, D., & Herrera, J. (2009). Knowledge management tools: convergences towards organizational learning. *Cuban Journal of Agricultural Science, 43* (1), 1-13.

[23]   http://www.geocities.ws/msimoz2/ihai/SKA011.pdf.

24]   Mijangos Noh, Juan Carlos, & Manzo Cabrera, Karla Sugey. (2012). Knowledge management of three consolidated academic bodies in the educational area. Sinéctica, (38), 1-13. Retrieved July 18, 2019, from http://www.scielo.org.mx/scielo.php?script=sci_arttext&pid=S1665-109X2012000100006&lng=es&tlng=es.

25] CANALS, Agustí (2003). "La gestión del conocimiento (Knowledge management). In: Acto de presentación del libro Gestión del conocimiento (2003: Barcelona). UOC. Date of consultation: 12/09/17]. <http://www.uoc.edu/dt/20251/index.html>

26] Gestión en el Tercer Milenio, Rev. de Investigación de la Facultad de Ciencias Administrativas, UNMSM (Vol. 9, No. 17, Lima, July 2006).

[30] Polo, A. Knowledge Management. Consulted on August 13, 2018 at www: https://www.gestiopolis.com/pasos-la-gestion-del-conocimiento/

31] Torres, M., Paz, K., & Salazar, F. (2006). Sample size for market research. *Universidad Rafael Landívar: Boletín electrónico [online]. Consultado 6.04. 2015] Available at: http://www. tec. url. edu. gt/boletin/URL_02_BAS02. pdf.*

[32] http://www.monografias.com/trabajos58/principales-tipos-investigacion/principales-tipos-investigacion.shtml

[33] Oscar Castillero Mimenza. https://psicologiaymente.net/miscelanea/tipos-de-investigacion

34] María Dolors Bernabeu and María Cónsul. https://educrea.cl/aprendizaje-basado-en-problemas-el-metodo-abp/

[35] Julián Pérez Porto and María Merino. Published: 2014. Updated: 2016. Definition of: Definition of repository (https://definicion.de/repositorio/)

[36] http://tugimnasiacerebral.com/mapas-conceptuales-y-mentales/que-es-un-mapa-conceptual

37] Ureña, Y., & Quiñones, E., & Carruyo, N. (2016). INTELLECTUAL CAPITAL: STRATEGIC MODEL FOR QUALITY OF SERVICE IN INTELLIGENT ORGANIZATIONS. *Orbis. Revista Científica Ciencias Humanas, 12* (35), 3-17.

[38] https://es.slideshare.net/VictorMolina2/km-andreu-wiigfb

39] K. Wiig; Foundations of Knowledge Management: Thinking about Thinking - How People and Organizations Create, Represent and Use Knowledge, Volume 1 of the Knowledge Management Series, Arlington, TX: Schema Press, France, 1993.

40] Brooking, A. (2004). Intellectual capital: The main asset of the companies of the third millennium. Barcelona: Paidós.

41] Nonaka, I., & Takeuchi, H. (1999). The Knowledge-Creating Organization: How Japanese Companies Create the Dynamics of Innovation. Mexico: Oxford University Press.

42] F. Guadamillas; La gestión del conocimiento como recurso estratégico en un proceso de mejora continua, Alta Dirección, 217, pp199-209, 2001

43] Rodríguez Gómez, D. (2006). Models for the creation and management of knowledge: a theoretical approach. *EDUCAR, 37,* 25-39.

44] G. Sammour, The role of knowledge management and e-learning in professional development. Knowledge and Learning, 4 (5), pp 465-477, 2008

45] M. Careaga, A. Avendaño. Modelo gestión del conocimiento para plataformas de docencia universitaria mixta, (GC+TIC/DUM), nuevas ideas en informática educativa, p.p 355-376, 2009.

46]   Extracted   from   https://smarterworkspaces.kyocera.es/blog/las-bases-datos-documentales/ on 02-07-19

47] Cazau, P. (2006). Introduction to social science research. Buenos Aires, 27.

48] Básico, B., & Guerrero, A. M. G. F. (2004). Research Methodology.

49] Morales, F. (2012). Learn about 3 types of research: Descriptive, Exploratory, and Explanatory. Recovered on, 11.

50] Extracted from: https://www.youtube.com/watch?v=AJcy4eZMwWM

51]   Extracted: https://christmo99.wordpress.com/2008/07/15/conocimiento-tacito-y-explicito/ on 05-08-19

52]   Taken   from   the   web   address: https://educrea.cl/aprendizaje-basado-en-problemas-el-metodo-abp/ on 06-08-19

53] Extracted from: http://gestionandomiconocimiento.blogspot.com/ on 06-08-19

Glossary

Knowledge-based societies

"It visualizes a social and economic development based on processes of sharing people's knowledge to create value and innovations (learning processes) that are translated into products and services and, ultimately, into well-being for the citizen". [6]

Concept maps

"A concept map is a learning tool based on the graphic representation of a certain topic through the schematization of the concepts that compose it. These concepts are written in a hierarchical way within geometric figures such as ovals or boxes, which are connected to each other through lines and linking words. The use of concept maps allows organizing and understanding ideas in a meaningful way. The origin of this tool lies in the 1960s with the theories on the psychology of meaningful learning developed by David Ausubel and was put into practice in 1970 by Joseph Novak". [36]

"Tacit knowledge" [51]

"It is the one that remains in an <u>unconscious </u>level, it is disarticulated and we implement and execute it in a mechanical way without realizing its content, it is something that we know but it is very difficult to explain". [51]

"Explicit knowledge" [Wikipedia]

"Explicit knowledge" refers to that which has been or can be articulated, codified and stored in some type of medium. It can be transmitted immediately to others.

Information contained in encyclopedias is a good example of explicit knowledge. [Wikipedia]

Intellectual capital

"Within an organization or company, intellectual capital is the intellectual knowledge of that organization, the intangible information (which is not visible, and therefore is not collected anywhere) that it possesses and that can produce value". [Wikipedia]

Information repository

"Repository" is a term that has its etymological root in repositorium, a Latin word. A repository is a space that is used to store different things. The idea of a repository can be associated with the concept of an archive or a repository. In a repository, something is stored, which may be material (physical) or symbolic. In this sense, nowadays digital databases and various computer systems are often referred to as repositories. Nowadays the usual thing is to store all the information digitally with the relevant software and this needs to offer customization and interoperability, among other things". [35]

Telematic networks

"A telematic network makes it possible to offer or have information at a distance, as well as to facilitate and make communication possible. You can make use of services or programs that are available on certain computers on the network which are called servers. Author: Jenny Danelly Quevedo Matías

Intranet

"Internal computer network of a company or organization, based on Internet standards, in which computers are connected to one or more servers. [Wikipedia]

Problem-based learning

"Problem-based learning (PBL) is a student-centered learning method in which students acquire knowledge, skills, and attitudes through real-life situations. Its purpose is to form students capable of analyzing and facing problems in the same way they will during their professional activity, that is, valuing and integrating the knowledge that will lead them to the acquisition of professional skills". [52]

Documentary databases

"Documentary databases are designed to store semi-structured data, such as documents. Unlike traditional relational databases, the schema for each non-relational document (NoSQL) can vary, offering developers, database administrators, and IT professionals more flexibility in organizing and storing application data, as well as a reduction in the storage required for optional values. Documentary databases are a modern way of storing data in a simple format instead of the simple rows and columns of relational databases. This allows data to be expressed in its natural form". [46]

Expert Directory

"It is defined as a list of "all experts possessing knowledge at an initial, intermediate or higher level, allows to identify which people in the business can help solve problems, participate in initiatives among others. It is essential to be clear that this directory becomes an objective map supported by the knowledge map data". [53]

QUESTIONNAIRE APPLIED TO THE SAMPLE:

1.   Are you familiar with the concept of knowledge management?

2.   Describe the concept of implicit knowledge

3.   Describe the concept of explicit knowledge

4.   Mention the knowledge management tools or instruments you have used in your laboratory sessions

5.   Have you used a history of results in your lab sessions?

6.   Have you used a documentary database in your lab sessions?

7.   Have you used the intranet in your lab sessions?

8.   Do you belong to a student community?

9.   Have you used an expert directory in your lab sessions?

10.   In your laboratory sessions, have you used computer tools that make group work possible?

11.   have you participated in knowledge fairs?

12.   What computer resources have you used in your lab sessions?

13.   In your lab sessions, have you conducted research on any academic subject of interest to you?

14.   In your laboratory sessions, have you had communication or contact with national or foreign scientists?

15.   In your lab sessions, have you had access to a communication platform that has allowed you to communicate or interact with your fellow students regarding your research?

16.   In your laboratory sessions, have you carried out simulations of extreme or high-precision experiments?

17.   Have the results, products or conclusions of your laboratory work been stored in a DB that has served the other generations of students and faculty members of the faculty?

18.   Add any comments you feel are necessary regarding the topic of the survey.